THE ULTIMATE *2024*

BREVILLE SMART OVEN

AIR FRYER

Cookbook for Beginners

1800 Days of Easy, Delicious Recipes to Delight Your Taste Buds, Healthy Eating for Beginners and Pros, with Colorful Pictures.

Table of Contents

Introduction..4

Chapter 1: Breakfast.......................................7

Chapter 2: Appetizers & Snacks.....................23

Chapter 3: Main Courses..............................37

Chapter 4: Side Dishes................................55

Chapter 5: Desserts.....................................67

Chapter 6: Healthy Dishes............................77

Chapter 7: Entertaining & Holiday...............89

Appendix 1: Measurement Conversion Chart.........100

Index...101

INTRODUCTION

Welcome to the world of effortless, gourmet cooking with the Breville Smart Oven Air Fryer Pro! Whether you're a seasoned chef or a home cook eager to explore new culinary horizons, this versatile appliance is about to become your new kitchen companion. With its wide range of functions, from air frying and roasting to baking and dehydrating, the Breville Smart Oven Air Fryer Pro empowers you to create delicious meals with ease and precision.

In today's fast-paced world, finding time to prepare healthy and tasty meals can be a challenge. That's where the Breville Smart Oven Air Fryer Pro shines. It's not just another countertop oven—it's an all-in-one kitchen powerhouse that can replace multiple appliances, save you time, and open up endless culinary possibilities. Imagine crispy air-fried snacks, perfectly roasted meats, and golden-baked desserts—all made in one compact oven.

This cookbook is designed to help you get the most out of your Breville Smart Oven Air Fryer Pro, guiding you through a variety of recipes that showcase its capabilities. From quick breakfasts to impressive holiday dishes, you'll find recipes that are not only delicious but also simple to prepare, making your time in the kitchen more enjoyable and less stressful.

Whether you're looking to whip up a quick weekday dinner or impress guests with a gourmet spread, this cookbook has you covered. We'll start with an overview of the appliance, so you can become familiar with its features and functions. Then, we'll dive into the recipes, organized by meals and occasions, so you can easily find what you need.

So, let's get started on this culinary journey! With the Breville Smart Oven Air Fryer Pro by your side, cooking has never been easier—or more delicious.

How to Use the Breville Smart Oven Pro

The Breville Smart Oven Air Fryer Pro is a sophisticated kitchen appliance that combines several cooking functions into one powerful machine. With its intuitive controls and advanced technology, you can easily prepare a wide range of dishes, from crispy fries to perfectly roasted meats. Here's a step-by-step guide to help you get started and make the most of your Breville Smart Oven Air Fryer Pro.

1. Getting Familiar with the Appliance

The Breville Smart Oven Air Fryer Pro is equipped with a variety of features designed to make cooking easier and more efficient:

- Element IQ® Technology: This smart feature distributes heat across four independent quartz elements to ensure precise and even cooking. The heat is automatically adjusted depending on the cooking mode selected.
- LCD Display: The easy-to-read display allows you to select cooking functions, set the temperature, and adjust the cooking time with just a few taps.
- Interior Oven Light: The built-in light automatically turns on when the door is opened, making it easy to check on your food without interrupting the cooking process.

2. Using the Control Panel

The control panel on your Breville Smart Oven Air Fryer Pro is straightforward and user-friendly. Here's a quick overview of the main controls:

- Function Dial: Use this dial to select from a variety of cooking functions, including Air Fry, Roast, Bake, Toast, Broil, Reheat, Warm, and more.
- Temperature and Time Dials: These dials allow you to set your desired cooking temperature and time. For certain functions, such as Toast and Bagel, you can also adjust the browning level.
- Start/Cancel Button: Press this button to start or cancel cooking at any time.

3. Preheating the Oven

For most recipes, it's important to preheat the oven to the desired temperature before cooking. To preheat:
- Turn the Function Dial to select the cooking function you want to use.
- Use the Temperature Dial to set the desired temperature.
- Press the Start button to begin preheating. The oven will alert you when it has reached the set temperature.

4. Cooking Functions Overview

- Air Fry: Achieve crispy, golden results with little to no oil. Ideal for fries, chicken wings, and other fried favorites.
- Roast: Perfect for meats, vegetables, and poultry, this function provides even heat distribution for tender and flavorful results.
- Bake: Bake your favorite cookies, cakes, and pastries with precision. The Bake function ensures even browning and consistent results.
- Broil: Use the Broil function to sear meats or create a crispy top layer on casseroles and gratins.
- Toast and Bagel: These functions allow you to toast bread or bagels to your preferred level of crispness.
- Reheat and Warm: Easily reheat leftovers or keep dishes warm until you're ready to serve.
- Dehydrate: Gently dry out fruits, vegetables, and even meats for homemade snacks like dried fruit or beef jerky.
- Slow Cook: The oven also doubles as a slow cooker, perfect for tender stews and braised dishes.

5. Accessories and Their Uses

Your Breville Smart Oven Air Fryer Pro comes with several accessories designed to enhance your cooking experience:

- Air Fryer Basket: Use this mesh basket for air frying. The elevated design allows hot air to circulate around the food for even crisping.
- Wire Rack: This rack can be used for toasting, baking, or broiling. It can be positioned at different levels depending on the recipe.
- Baking Pan: The baking pan is ideal for roasting meats, baking cakes, or catching drips from the air fryer basket.
- Pizza Pan: Designed specifically for making pizzas, this pan ensures an evenly cooked, crispy crust.

6. Cleaning and Maintenance

To keep your Breville Smart Oven Air Fryer Pro in top condition:

- Unplug the Oven: Always unplug the appliance before cleaning.
- Wipe Down the Exterior: Use a damp cloth to clean the exterior surfaces. Avoid using abrasive cleaners.
- Clean the Interior: Remove any food residue from the interior with a soft cloth or sponge. For stubborn stains, use a non-abrasive cleaner.
- Clean Accessories: Most accessories are dishwasher safe. Check the manual for specific care instructions.

7. Safety Tips

- Always use oven mitts when handling hot accessories or opening the oven door.
- Place the oven on a flat, stable surface with enough clearance around it to prevent overheating.
- Avoid using the oven with wet hands or on wet surfaces to prevent electrical shock.

With these instructions, you're well on your way to mastering the Breville Smart Oven Air Fryer Pro. Whether you're air frying, roasting, baking, or dehydrating, this appliance will help you achieve delicious, consistent results every time.

Chapter I: Breakfast

Avocado Toast with Poached Egg

Prep: 10 Minutes | Cook: 8 Minutes | Makes: 2 Servings

Ingredients:

- 2 slices of whole-grain bread
- 1 ripe avocado, mashed
- 2 large eggs
- 1 tbsp lemon juice
- Salt and pepper to taste
- Red pepper flakes (optional)
- Fresh herbs for garnish (optional)

Directions:

1. Preheat your Breville Smart Oven Air Fryer Pro using the Toast function, setting the browning level to your preference.

2. Place the bread slices on the wire rack and toast until golden and crispy.

3. Meanwhile, bring a small pot of water to a gentle simmer. Crack the eggs into separate cups and gently slide them into the simmering water to poach for 3-4 minutes, or until the whites are set.

4. While the eggs are poaching, mash the avocado in a bowl with lemon juice, salt, and pepper.

5. Spread the mashed avocado evenly on the toasted bread slices.

6. Top each slice with a poached egg. Sprinkle with red pepper flakes and fresh herbs if desired.

7. Serve immediately and enjoy!

Tip: For a bit of extra crunch, try adding some toasted seeds or nuts on top.

Crispy Sweet Potato Hash with Bacon

Prep: 15 Minutes | Cook: 20 Minutes | Makes: 4 Servings

Ingredients:

- 2 large sweet potatoes, peeled and diced
- 4 slices of bacon, chopped
- 1 small onion, diced
- 1 red bell pepper, diced
- 1 tsp smoked paprika
- 1 tsp garlic powder
- Salt and pepper to taste
- Fresh parsley for garnish

Directions:

1. Preheat your Breville Smart Oven Air Fryer Pro to 400°F using the Air Fry function.

2. In a large bowl, toss the diced sweet potatoes with smoked paprika, garlic powder, salt, and pepper.

3. Place the bacon and onion in the air fryer basket. Cook for 5 minutes until the bacon begins to crisp.

4. Add the seasoned sweet potatoes and red bell pepper to the basket, tossing to combine with the bacon and onion.

5. Air fry for an additional 15 minutes, shaking the basket halfway through to ensure even cooking.

6. Once the sweet potatoes are crispy and the bacon is fully cooked, transfer the hash to a serving platter.

7. Garnish with fresh parsley and serve hot.

Tip: Add a fried egg on top for a more filling breakfast.

Baked Berry Oatmeal Cups

Prep: 10 Minutes | Cook: 25 Minutes | Makes: 6 Servings

Ingredients:

- 2 cups rolled oats
- 1 tsp baking powder
- 1 tsp cinnamon
- 1/4 tsp salt
- 1 cup milk (dairy or plant-based)
- 1/4 cup maple syrup
- 1 large egg
- 2 tbsp melted coconut oil
- 1 tsp vanilla extract
- 1 cup mixed berries (blueberries, raspberries, etc.)

Directions:

1. Preheat your Breville Smart Oven Air Fryer Pro to 350°F using the Bake function.
2. In a large bowl, mix the oats, baking powder, cinnamon, and salt.
3. In another bowl, whisk together the milk, maple syrup, egg, melted coconut oil, and vanilla extract.
4. Pour the wet ingredients into the dry ingredients and mix until well combined. Fold in the mixed berries.
5. Divide the mixture evenly among a greased muffin tin, filling each cup about 3/4 full.
6. Bake in the oven for 20-25 minutes, or until the oatmeal cups are golden and set.
7. Allow the oatmeal cups to cool slightly before removing them from the tin. Serve warm or store for later.

Tip: These oatmeal cups can be made ahead and reheated in the oven for a quick breakfast on busy mornings.

Breakfast Burritos

Prep: 10 Minutes | Cook: 10 Minutes | Makes: 4 Servings

Ingredients:

- 4 large flour tortillas
- 4 large eggs, scrambled
- 1 cup cooked breakfast sausage, crumbled
- 1 cup shredded cheddar cheese
- 1/2 cup diced tomatoes
- 1/4 cup chopped green onions
- Salsa and sour cream for serving

Directions:

1. Preheat your Breville Smart Oven Air Fryer Pro to 375°F using the Air Fry function.
2. Lay out the tortillas and evenly distribute the scrambled eggs, sausage, cheese, diced tomatoes, and green onions in the center of each tortilla.
3. Roll up each tortilla tightly, folding in the sides as you go, to form a burrito.
4. Place the burritos seam-side down in the air fryer basket. Air fry for 8-10 minutes, or until the tortillas are golden and crispy.
5. Serve the burritos hot with salsa and sour cream on the side.

Tip: Customize your burritos by adding ingredients like avocado, jalapeños, or black beans.

Apple Cinnamon Pancake Bites

Prep: 10 Minutes | Cook: 12 Minutes | Makes: 4 Servings

Ingredients:

- 1 cup pancake mix
- 1/2 cup milk
- 1 large egg
- 1/2 tsp cinnamon
- 1/2 cup finely diced apple
- Maple syrup for serving

Directions:

1. Preheat your Breville Smart Oven Air Fryer Pro to 350°F using the Bake function.
2. In a mixing bowl, combine the pancake mix, milk, egg, and cinnamon until smooth.
3. Gently fold in the diced apple.
4. Grease a mini muffin tin and fill each cup about 3/4 full with the pancake batter.
5. Bake in the oven for 10-12 minutes, or until the pancake bites are golden and set.
6. Remove the pancake bites from the muffin tin and serve warm with maple syrup.

Tip: For an extra touch of sweetness, dust the pancake bites with powdered sugar before serving.

Banana Nut Muffins

Prep: 15 Minutes | Cook: 15 Minutes | Makes: 12 Muffins

Ingredients:

- 2 ripe bananas, mashed
- 1/3 cup melted butter
- 1/2 cup sugar
- 1 large egg, beaten
- 1 tsp vanilla extract
- 1 tsp baking soda
- 1/4 tsp salt
- 1 1/2 cups all-purpose flour
- 1/2 cup chopped walnuts

Directions:

1. Preheat your Breville Smart Oven Air Fryer Pro to 350°F using the Bake function.
2. In a large bowl, mix the mashed bananas and melted butter until well combined.
3. Stir in the sugar, beaten egg, and vanilla extract.
4. Sprinkle the baking soda and salt over the mixture and stir in.
5. Gently fold in the flour and chopped walnuts until just combined.
6. Grease a muffin tin and fill each cup about 3/4 full with the batter.
7. Bake for 12-15 minutes, or until a toothpick inserted into the center of a muffin comes out clean.
8. Let the muffins cool slightly before removing them from the tin. Serve warm.

Tip: Add a sprinkle of extra chopped walnuts on top before baking for a crunchy finish.

Veggie Breakfast Frittata

Prep: 10 Minutes | Cook: 20 Minutes | Makes: 4 Servings

Ingredients:

- 6 large eggs
- 1/4 cup milk
- 1/2 cup shredded cheddar cheese
- 1/2 cup diced bell pepper
- 1/2 cup diced zucchini
- 1/4 cup diced onion
- Salt and pepper to taste
- Fresh herbs for garnish (optional)

Directions:

1. Preheat your Breville Smart Oven Air Fryer Pro to 375°F using the Bake function.
2. In a large bowl, whisk together the eggs, milk, and a pinch of salt and pepper.
3. Stir in the shredded cheese, bell pepper, zucchini, and onion.
4. Pour the mixture into a greased baking dish that fits inside the air fryer basket.
5. Bake for 18-20 minutes, or until the frittata is set and the top is lightly golden.
6. Allow the frittata to cool slightly before slicing. Garnish with fresh herbs if desired.

Tip: You can customize this frittata by adding your favorite veggies, meats, or cheeses.

Churro Waffles

Prep: 10 Minutes | Cook: 8 Minutes | Makes: 4 Waffles

Ingredients:

- 1 cup waffle mix
- 3/4 cup milk
- 1 large egg
- 2 tbsp melted butter
- 1/4 cup sugar
- 1 tsp ground cinnamon

Directions:

1. Preheat your Breville Smart Oven Air Fryer Pro to 360°F using the Air Fry function.
2. In a mixing bowl, combine the waffle mix, milk, egg, and melted butter until smooth.
3. Pour the batter into a greased waffle maker and cook until golden brown.
4. In a small bowl, mix together the sugar and cinnamon.
5. Once the waffles are cooked, lightly brush them with melted butter and sprinkle generously with the cinnamon-sugar mixture.
6. Place the waffles in the air fryer basket and air fry for 2-3 minutes to crisp up the outside.
7. Serve the churro waffles warm with your favorite toppings, such as whipped cream or fresh fruit.

Tip: For an indulgent treat, drizzle some chocolate sauce over the waffles before serving.

Baked Greek Yogurt and Berry Parfaits

Prep: 5 Minutes | Cook: 10 Minutes | Makes: 4 Servings

Ingredients:

- 2 cups Greek yogurt
- 1/4 cup honey
- 1 tsp vanilla extract
- 1 cup mixed berries (blueberries, strawberries, raspberries)
- 1/2 cup granola
- Fresh mint leaves for garnish (optional)

Directions:

1. Preheat your Breville Smart Oven Air Fryer Pro to 350°F using the Bake function.
2. In a mixing bowl, combine the Greek yogurt, honey, and vanilla extract.
3. Divide the yogurt mixture evenly among small, oven-safe ramekins.
4. Top each ramekin with mixed berries.
5. Bake for 10 minutes until the yogurt is slightly warm and the berries are softened.
6. Remove from the oven and let cool slightly.
7. Sprinkle with granola and garnish with fresh mint leaves if desired. Serve immediately.

Tip: For added crunch, toast the granola in the air fryer for a few minutes before sprinkling it on top.

Breakfast Pizza

Prep: 10 Minutes | Cook: 12 Minutes | Makes: 4 Servings

Ingredients:

- 1 pre-made pizza dough
- 1/4 cup pizza sauce
- 1 cup shredded mozzarella cheese
- 4 large eggs
- 1/2 cup cooked breakfast sausage, crumbled
- 1/4 cup diced bell pepper
- Fresh basil leaves for garnish (optional)

Directions:

1. Preheat your Breville Smart Oven Air Fryer Pro to 400°F using the Air Fry function.
2. Roll out the pizza dough on a floured surface to fit the air fryer basket.
3. Spread the pizza sauce evenly over the dough, leaving a small border around the edges.
4. Sprinkle the shredded mozzarella cheese over the sauce.
5. Carefully crack the eggs onto the pizza, spacing them evenly.
6. Scatter the crumbled sausage and diced bell pepper around the eggs.
7. Air fry for 10-12 minutes, or until the crust is golden and the eggs are cooked to your liking.
8. Garnish with fresh basil leaves and serve immediately.

Tip: For a more runny yolk, cook the pizza for a shorter time and keep an eye on the eggs.

Cinnamon Roll Bites

Prep: 10 Minutes | Cook: 8 Minutes | Makes: 4 Servings

Ingredients:

- 1 can refrigerated cinnamon roll dough
- 1/4 cup melted butter
- 1/4 cup sugar
- 1 tsp ground cinnamon
- Icing (included with cinnamon rolls)

Directions:

1. Preheat your Breville Smart Oven Air Fryer Pro to 350°F using the Air Fry function.
2. Cut each cinnamon roll into bite-sized pieces.
3. In a small bowl, mix the sugar and cinnamon together.
4. Dip each cinnamon roll bite into the melted butter, then roll it in the cinnamon-sugar mixture.
5. Place the bites in the air fryer basket in a single layer. Air fry for 6-8 minutes, or until golden brown and cooked through.
6. Drizzle the included icing over the warm cinnamon roll bites and serve immediately.

Tip: For an extra indulgence, serve with a side of warm caramel sauce for dipping.

Baked Eggs in Avocado

Prep: 5 Minutes | Cook: 15 Minutes | Makes: 2 Servings

Ingredients:

- 2 ripe avocados
- 4 large eggs
- Salt and pepper to taste
- Red pepper flakes (optional)
- Fresh herbs for garnish (optional)

Directions:

1. Preheat your Breville Smart Oven Air Fryer Pro to 375°F using the Bake function.
2. Cut the avocados in half and remove the pits. Scoop out a small amount of the flesh to create a larger cavity for the egg.
3. Place the avocado halves on a baking dish that fits inside the air fryer basket.
4. Carefully crack an egg into each avocado half, being careful not to overflow.
5. Season with salt, pepper, and red pepper flakes if desired.
6. Bake for 12-15 minutes, or until the eggs are cooked to your preferred doneness.
7. Garnish with fresh herbs and serve immediately.

Tip: Add a sprinkle of cheese or a drizzle of hot sauce for extra flavor.

French Toast Sticks

Prep: 10 Minutes | Cook: 8 Minutes | Makes: 4 Servings

Ingredients:

- 4 slices of thick bread (brioche or Texas toast)
- 2 large eggs
- 1/4 cup milk
- 1 tsp vanilla extract
- 1/2 tsp ground cinnamon
- 1/4 cup sugar
- Maple syrup for serving

Directions:

1. Preheat your Breville Smart Oven Air Fryer Pro to 350°F using the Air Fry function.
2. Cut each slice of bread into 3-4 sticks.
3. In a shallow bowl, whisk together the eggs, milk, vanilla extract, and cinnamon.
4. Dip each bread stick into the egg mixture, making sure to coat all sides.
5. Place the coated bread sticks in the air fryer basket in a single layer. Air fry for 6-8 minutes, flipping halfway through, until golden brown and crispy.
6. In a small bowl, mix together the sugar and a little extra cinnamon.
7. Roll the warm French toast sticks in the cinnamon-sugar mixture.
8. Serve immediately with maple syrup for dipping.

Tip: These can be made ahead and reheated in the air fryer for a quick breakfast on busy mornings.

Baked Quinoa Breakfast Cups

Prep: 10 Minutes | Cook: 20 Minutes | Makes: 6 Servings

Ingredients:

- 1 cup cooked quinoa
- 4 large eggs
- 1/2 cup shredded cheddar cheese
- 1/4 cup diced bell pepper
- 1/4 cup diced spinach
- Salt and pepper to taste
- 1/4 tsp garlic powder

Directions:

1. Preheat your Breville Smart Oven Air Fryer Pro to 375°F using the Bake function.
2. In a large bowl, whisk together the eggs, salt, pepper, and garlic powder.
3. Stir in the cooked quinoa, shredded cheese, bell pepper, and spinach until well combined.
4. Grease a muffin tin and fill each cup about 3/4 full with the quinoa mixture.
5. Bake for 18-20 minutes, or until the cups are set and lightly golden on top.
6. Allow the quinoa cups to cool slightly before removing them from the tin. Serve warm.

Tip: These cups can be made in advance and stored in the refrigerator for up to three days. Reheat in the oven or air fryer before serving.

Breakfast Quesadillas

Prep: 10 Minutes | Cook: 10 Minutes | Makes: 2 Servings

Ingredients:
- 2 large flour tortillas
- 4 large eggs, scrambled
- 1/2 cup cooked breakfast sausage, crumbled
- 1/2 cup shredded cheddar cheese
- 1/4 cup diced tomatoes
- 1/4 cup diced green onions
- Salsa and sour cream for serving

Directions:
1. Preheat your Breville Smart Oven Air Fryer Pro to 375°F using the Air Fry function.
2. Lay one tortilla flat and evenly distribute the scrambled eggs, sausage, cheese, tomatoes, and green onions.
3. Top with the second tortilla, pressing down gently to seal.
4. Place the quesadilla in the air fryer basket and air fry for 8-10 minutes, flipping halfway through, until the tortilla is golden and crispy, and the cheese is melted.
5. Remove from the air fryer and cut into wedges.
6. Serve warm with salsa and sour cream on the side.

Tip: For added flavor, spread a thin layer of refried beans on the bottom tortilla before adding the fillings.

Blueberry Pancake Bites

Prep: 10 Minutes | Cook: 12 Minutes | Makes: 4 Servings

Ingredients:
- 1 cup pancake mix
- 3/4 cup milk
- 1 large egg
- 1 tsp vanilla extract
- 1/2 cup fresh or frozen blueberries
- Maple syrup for serving

Directions:
1. Preheat your Breville Smart Oven Air Fryer Pro to 350°F using the Bake function.
2. In a mixing bowl, combine the pancake mix, milk, egg, and vanilla extract until smooth.
3. Gently fold in the blueberries.
4. Grease a mini muffin tin and fill each cup about 3/4 full with the pancake batter.
5. Bake in the oven for 10-12 minutes, or until the pancake bites are golden and cooked through.
6. Remove the pancake bites from the tin and serve warm with maple syrup.

Tip: Add a sprinkle of powdered sugar on top for an extra touch of sweetness.

Baked Ham and Cheese Breakfast Sliders

Prep: 10 Minutes | Cook: 15 Minutes | Makes: 6 Servings

Ingredients:

- 12 slider buns
- 6 slices of ham
- 6 slices of Swiss cheese
- 4 large eggs, scrambled
- 2 tbsp melted butter
- 1 tbsp Dijon mustard
- 1 tsp poppy seeds
- 1/2 tsp garlic powder

Directions:

1. Preheat your Breville Smart Oven Air Fryer Pro to 375°F using the Bake function.
2. Slice the slider buns in half horizontally and place the bottom halves in a baking dish.
3. Layer the ham, scrambled eggs, and Swiss cheese on top of the bottom halves of the buns.
4. Place the top halves of the buns on the sliders.
5. In a small bowl, mix together the melted butter, Dijon mustard, poppy seeds, and garlic powder.
6. Brush the butter mixture over the tops of the sliders.
7. Bake for 12-15 minutes, or until the sliders are golden and the cheese is melted.

Tip: These sliders are perfect for a crowd and can be made ahead and reheated.

Sweet Potato and Black Bean Tacos

Prep: 15 Minutes | Cook: 20 Minutes | Makes: 4 Servings

Ingredients:

- 2 medium sweet potatoes, peeled and diced
- 1 tbsp olive oil
- 1 tsp smoked paprika
- 1/2 tsp cumin
- Salt and pepper to taste
- 1 cup canned black beans, drained and rinsed
- 4 large eggs, scrambled
- 8 small flour tortillas
- 1/4 cup crumbled feta cheese
- Fresh cilantro for garnish

Directions:

1. Preheat your Breville Smart Oven Air Fryer Pro to 400°F using the Air Fry function.
2. Toss the diced sweet potatoes with olive oil, smoked paprika, cumin, salt, and pepper.
3. Place the sweet potatoes in the air fryer basket and cook for 15-20 minutes, shaking the basket halfway through, until tender and crispy.
4. In the last few minutes of cooking, warm the tortillas in the oven using the Warm function.
5. Assemble the tacos by filling each tortilla with sweet potatoes, black beans, and scrambled eggs.
6. Top with crumbled feta cheese and fresh cilantro.

Tip: For a spicy kick, add a drizzle of hot sauce or salsa.

GRANOLA-STUFFED APPLES

Prep: 10 Minutes | Cook: 20 Minutes | Makes: 4 Servings

Ingredients:
- 4 large apples, cored
- 1/2 cup granola
- 1/4 cup chopped nuts (e.g., walnuts or pecans)
- 2 tbsp honey
- 1 tsp cinnamon
- 2 tbsp butter, cut into small pieces

Directions:
1. Preheat your Breville Smart Oven Air Fryer Pro to 350°F using the Bake function.
2. In a small bowl, mix together the granola, chopped nuts, honey, and cinnamon.
3. Stuff the mixture into the cored apples, pressing it down firmly.
4. Place a small piece of butter on top of each stuffed apple.
5. Place the apples in a baking dish that fits in the air fryer basket.
6. Bake for 20 minutes, or until the apples are tender and the topping is golden.
7. Serve warm, optionally with a scoop of yogurt or a drizzle of extra honey.

Tip: These can also be served as a dessert with a scoop of vanilla ice cream.

TAQUITOS

Prep: 15 Minutes | Cook: 10 Minutes | Makes: 4 Servings

Ingredients:
- 8 small corn tortillas
- 4 large eggs, scrambled
- 1/2 cup cooked chorizo or breakfast sausage
- 1/2 cup shredded cheddar cheese
- 1/4 cup salsa
- Cooking spray

Directions:
1. Preheat your Breville Smart Oven Air Fryer Pro to 375°F using the Air Fry function.
2. Warm the tortillas in the microwave for a few seconds to make them pliable.
3. Place a spoonful of scrambled eggs, chorizo, and shredded cheese in the center of each tortilla.
4. Roll up the tortillas tightly to form taquitos.
5. Place the taquitos seam-side down in the air fryer basket and lightly spray them with cooking spray.
6. Air fry for 8-10 minutes, or until the taquitos are golden and crispy.
7. Serve with salsa for dipping.

Tip: For added crunch, sprinkle a little more cheese on top of the taquitos before air frying.

STUFFED BELL PEPPERS

Prep: 10 Minutes | Cook: 15 Minutes | Makes: 4 Servings

Ingredients:
- 4 large bell peppers (any color), tops cut off and seeds removed
- 4 large eggs
- 1/2 cup cooked breakfast sausage, crumbled
- 1/2 cup shredded cheddar cheese
- 1/4 cup diced tomatoes
- 1/4 cup diced onions
- Salt and pepper to taste
- Fresh parsley for garnish (optional)

Directions:
1. Preheat your Breville Smart Oven Air Fryer Pro to 375°F using the Bake function.
2. In a bowl, mix the cooked sausage, cheese, diced tomatoes, and onions.
3. Stuff each bell pepper with the sausage mixture, leaving room at the top for the egg.
4. Crack an egg into each bell pepper, on top of the sausage mixture.
5. Place the stuffed bell peppers in a baking dish that fits inside the air fryer basket.
6. Bake for 15-18 minutes, or until the egg whites are set and the yolk reaches your preferred level of doneness.
7. Garnish with fresh parsley and serve immediately.

Tip: You can also add a sprinkle of extra cheese on top before baking for an extra cheesy finish.

BAKED BANANA AND OAT BARS

Prep: 10 Minutes | Cook: 25 Minutes | Makes: 6 Servings

Ingredients:
- 2 ripe bananas, mashed
- 2 cups rolled oats
- 1/4 cup peanut butter
- 1/4 cup honey
- 1/4 cup chopped nuts (e.g., almonds or walnuts)
- 1/2 tsp cinnamon
- 1/4 cup dark chocolate chips (optional)

Directions:
1. Preheat your Breville Smart Oven Air Fryer Pro to 350°F using the Bake function.
2. In a large bowl, combine the mashed bananas, oats, peanut butter, honey, chopped nuts, and cinnamon.
3. If using, fold in the dark chocolate chips.
4. Press the mixture evenly into a greased baking dish that fits in the air fryer basket.
5. Bake for 20-25 minutes, or until the bars are golden and set.
6. Allow the bars to cool before cutting them into squares. Serve or store for later.

Tip: These bars make a great grab-and-go breakfast or snack.

Breakfast Egg Rolls

Prep: 15 Minutes | Cook: 10 Minutes | Makes: 4 Servings

Ingredients:

- 8 egg roll wrappers
- 4 large eggs, scrambled
- 1/2 cup cooked bacon, crumbled
- 1/2 cup shredded cheese (cheddar or mozzarella)
- 1/4 cup diced bell peppers
- Cooking spray

Directions:

1. Preheat your Breville Smart Oven Air Fryer Pro to 375°F using the Air Fry function.
2. Lay an egg roll wrapper on a flat surface. Place a spoonful of scrambled eggs, bacon, cheese, and diced bell peppers in the center.
3. Roll up the wrapper tightly, folding in the sides as you go to seal the egg roll.
4. Repeat with the remaining wrappers and filling.
5. Lightly spray the egg rolls with cooking spray and place them in the air fryer basket in a single layer.
6. Air fry for 8-10 minutes, turning halfway through, until the egg rolls are golden and crispy.
7. Serve hot with a side of salsa or your favorite dipping sauce.

Tip: For a vegetarian version, substitute the bacon with sautéed mushrooms or spinach.

Spinach and Feta Pockets

Prep: 15 Minutes | Cook: 15 Minutes | Makes: 4 Servings

Ingredients:

- 1 sheet puff pastry, thawed
- 1 cup fresh spinach, chopped
- 1/2 cup crumbled feta cheese
- 2 large eggs, beaten (one for filling, one for brushing)
- 1/4 cup diced onions
- Salt and pepper to taste

Directions:

1. Preheat your Breville Smart Oven Air Fryer Pro to 375°F using the Bake function.
2. In a bowl, mix the chopped spinach, feta cheese, diced onions, and one beaten egg. Season with salt and pepper.
3. Roll out the puff pastry sheet and cut it into 4 equal squares.
4. Place a spoonful of the spinach mixture in the center of each square.
5. Fold the pastry over the filling to form a triangle, sealing the edges by pressing with a fork.
6. Brush the tops of the pockets with the remaining beaten egg.
7. Place the pockets on a baking sheet and bake for 12-15 minutes, or until the pastry is golden and puffed.
8. Serve warm.

Tip: These pockets can be made ahead of time and reheated in the air fryer for a quick breakfast.

CROISSANT SANDWICHES

Prep: 10 Minutes | Cook: 8 Minutes | Makes: 4 Servings

Ingredients:

4 croissants, sliced in half
4 large eggs, scrambled
4 slices of ham or turkey
4 slices of cheddar cheese
1 tbsp butter, softened

Directions:

1. Preheat your Breville Smart Oven Air Fryer Pro to 350°F using the Air Fry function.
2. Lightly butter the inside of each croissant half.
3. Layer the bottom half of each croissant with scrambled eggs, a slice of ham or turkey, and a slice of cheddar cheese.
4. Place the top half of the croissant on each sandwich.
5. Place the sandwiches in the air fryer basket and air fry for 6-8 minutes, or until the croissants are golden and the cheese is melted.

Tip: For added flavor, spread a thin layer of Dijon mustard or mayo inside the croissant before assembling.

MAPLE PECAN FRENCH TOAST CASSEROLE

Prep: 15 Minutes | Cook: 25 Minutes | Makes: 6 Servings

Ingredients:

- 1 loaf of brioche or challah bread, cubed
- 4 large eggs
- 1 1/2 cups milk
- 1/2 cup heavy cream
- 1/4 cup maple syrup
- 1 tsp vanilla extract
- 1/2 tsp ground cinnamon
- 1/4 tsp nutmeg
- 1/2 cup chopped pecans
- Extra maple syrup for serving

Directions:

1. Preheat your Breville Smart Oven Air Fryer Pro to 350°F using the Bake function.
2. In a large bowl, whisk together the eggs, milk, heavy cream, maple syrup, vanilla extract, cinnamon, and nutmeg.
3. Add the cubed bread to the mixture and gently toss to coat the bread evenly. Let it sit for 10 minutes to absorb the liquid.
4. Grease a baking dish that fits inside the air fryer basket and pour the bread mixture into it.
5. Sprinkle the chopped pecans over the top.
6. Bake for 20-25 minutes, or until the casserole is golden brown and set in the center.
7. Let cool slightly before serving. Dust with powdered sugar and drizzle with extra maple syrup if desired.

Tip: For added flavor, mix some raisins or dried cranberries into the bread mixture before baking.

Chia Seed Pudding with Roasted Fruit

Prep: 10 Minutes (Plus Overnight Chilling) | Cook: 15 Minutes | Makes: 4 Servings

Ingredients:

- 1/2 cup chia seeds
- 2 cups almond milk (or any milk of your choice)
- 2 tbsp honey or maple syrup
- 1 tsp vanilla extract
- 2 cups mixed fruit (e.g., peaches, plums, or berries)
- 1 tbsp olive oil
- 1 tbsp brown sugar

Directions:

1. In a mixing bowl, whisk together the chia seeds, almond milk, honey, and vanilla extract. Let it sit for 5 minutes, then whisk again to prevent clumping.
2. Cover the mixture and refrigerate overnight or for at least 4 hours until the pudding thickens.
3. Preheat your Breville Smart Oven Air Fryer Pro to 375°F using the Air Fry function.
4. Toss the mixed fruit with olive oil and brown sugar. Spread the fruit on a baking sheet.
5. Roast the fruit in the air fryer for 12-15 minutes, or until softened and slightly caramelized.
6. To serve, divide the chia seed pudding into bowls and top with the roasted fruit.

Tip: You can also add a sprinkle of granola or nuts on top for added texture.

Baked Empanadas

Prep: 20 Minutes | Cook: 18 Minutes | Makes: 6 Servings

Ingredients:

- 1 package refrigerated pie dough
- 4 large eggs, scrambled
- 1/2 cup cooked chorizo or sausage, crumbled
- 1/2 cup shredded Monterey Jack cheese
- 1/4 cup diced onions
- 1 egg, beaten (for egg wash)

Directions:

1. Preheat your Breville Smart Oven Air Fryer Pro to 375°F using the Bake function.
2. Roll out the pie dough and cut out circles about 4-5 inches in diameter.
3. In the center of each circle, place a spoonful of scrambled eggs, crumbled chorizo, cheese, and diced onions.
4. Fold the dough over the filling to form a half-moon shape and press the edges together to seal. Crimp the edges with a fork.
5. Brush the tops of the empanadas with the beaten egg.
6. Place the empanadas in the air fryer basket and bake for 15-18 minutes, or until golden brown and cooked through.
7. Serve warm with salsa or guacamole.

Tip: These empanadas can be made ahead and frozen. Just pop them into the air fryer when ready to cook.

Strawberry Stuffed French Toast

Prep: 10 Minutes | Cook: 8 Minutes | Makes: 4 Servings

Ingredients:

- 8 slices of brioche or thick white bread
- 4 oz cream cheese, softened
- 1/4 cup strawberry jam
- 1 cup sliced fresh strawberries
- 4 large eggs
- 1/2 cup milk
- 1 tsp vanilla extract
- Powdered sugar for serving

Directions:

1. Preheat your Breville Smart Oven Air Fryer Pro to 350°F using the Air Fry function.
2. Spread cream cheese on one side of each slice of bread. Spread strawberry jam on the other side of four slices.
3. Place sliced strawberries on top of the jam and sandwich with the cream cheese slices.
4. In a shallow dish, whisk together the eggs, milk, and vanilla extract.
5. Dip each sandwich in the egg mixture, making sure to coat both sides.
6. Place the sandwiches in the air fryer basket and air fry for 6-8 minutes, flipping halfway through, until golden and crispy.
7. Serve warm with a dusting of powdered sugar and additional sliced strawberries.

Tip: You can substitute the strawberries with other fruits like blueberries or raspberries.

Mediterranean Flatbread

Prep: 10 Minutes | Cook: 12 Minutes | Makes: 4 Servings

Ingredients:

- 2 small flatbreads or naan
- 4 large eggs
- 1/2 cup crumbled feta cheese
- 1/4 cup chopped kalamata olives
- 1/4 cup diced cherry tomatoes
- 1/4 cup spinach, chopped
- 1 tbsp olive oil
- Salt and pepper to taste
- Fresh basil or oregano for garnish

Directions:

1. Preheat your Breville Smart Oven Air Fryer Pro to 400°F using the Bake function.
2. Place the flatbreads on a baking sheet. Drizzle with olive oil.
3. Scatter the feta cheese, olives, tomatoes, and spinach evenly over the flatbreads.
4. Carefully crack two eggs onto each flatbread.
5. Bake for 10-12 minutes, or until the eggs are cooked to your liking and the flatbreads are crispy.
6. Season with salt and pepper and garnish with fresh basil or oregano.

Tip: Add a sprinkle of red pepper flakes for a bit of heat.

Chapter 2: Appetizers & Snacks

Zucchini Fries

Prep: 15 Minutes | Cook: 12 Minutes | Makes: 4 Servings

Ingredients:

- 2 medium zucchini, cut into fries
- 1/2 cup all-purpose flour
- 2 large eggs, beaten
- 1 cup panko breadcrumbs
- 1/2 cup grated Parmesan cheese
- 1 tsp garlic powder
- 1 tsp Italian seasoning
- Salt and pepper to taste
- Marinara sauce for dipping

Directions:

1. Preheat your Breville Smart Oven Air Fryer Pro to 400°F using the Air Fry function.

2. In a shallow dish, place the flour. In another dish, place the beaten eggs. In a third dish, combine the panko breadcrumbs, Parmesan cheese, garlic powder, Italian seasoning, salt, and pepper.

3. Coat each zucchini fry in flour, then dip in the beaten eggs, and finally coat with the breadcrumb mixture.

4. Place the zucchini fries in the air fryer basket in a single layer.

5. Air fry for 10-12 minutes, turning halfway through, until the fries are golden and crispy.

6. Serve immediately with marinara sauce for dipping.

Tip: For extra crispiness, lightly spray the fries with cooking spray before air frying.

Spinach and Artichoke Dip

Prep: 10 Minutes | Cook: 20 Minutes | Makes: 6 Servings

Ingredients:

- 1 cup frozen spinach, thawed and drained
- 1 can (14 oz) artichoke hearts, drained and chopped
- 1/2 cup cream cheese, softened
- 1/2 cup sour cream
- 1/2 cup mayonnaise
- 1/2 cup grated Parmesan cheese
- 1/2 cup shredded mozzarella cheese
- 1 clove garlic, minced
- Salt and pepper to taste
- Pita chips or crackers for serving

Directions:

1. Preheat your Breville Smart Oven Air Fryer Pro to 375°F using the Bake function.

2. In a mixing bowl, combine the spinach, artichoke hearts, cream cheese, sour cream, mayonnaise, Parmesan cheese, mozzarella cheese, and garlic. Mix well until fully combined.

3. Season with salt and pepper to taste.

4. Transfer the mixture to a baking dish that fits in the air fryer basket.

5. Bake for 18-20 minutes, or until the dip is bubbly and golden on top.

6. Serve warm with pita chips or crackers.

Tip: You can make this dip ahead of time and bake just before serving.

Buffalo Cauliflower Bites

Prep: 10 Minutes | Cook: 15 Minutes | Makes: 4 Servings

Ingredients:

- 1 small head of cauliflower, cut into florets
- 1/2 cup all-purpose flour
- 1/2 cup water
- 1 tsp garlic powder
- 1/2 tsp smoked paprika
- Salt and pepper to taste
- 1/2 cup buffalo sauce
- 2 tbsp melted butter
- Ranch or blue cheese dressing for serving

Directions:

1. Preheat your Breville Smart Oven Air Fryer Pro to 375°F using the Air Fry function.
2. In a mixing bowl, whisk together the flour, water, garlic powder, smoked paprika, salt, and pepper to create a batter.
3. Toss the cauliflower florets in the batter until well coated.
4. Place the battered cauliflower in the air fryer basket in a single layer.
5. Air fry for 12-15 minutes, shaking the basket halfway through, until the cauliflower is golden and crispy.
6. In a separate bowl, mix the buffalo sauce and melted butter. Toss the cooked cauliflower bites in the sauce.
7. Serve immediately with ranch or blue cheese dressing for dipping.

Tip: For a spicier version, add a dash of hot sauce to the buffalo sauce mixture.

Jalapeño Poppers

Prep: 15 Minutes | Cook: 15 Minutes | Makes: 6 Servings

Ingredients:

- 12 large jalapeños, halved and seeded
- 8 oz cream cheese, softened
- 1/2 cup shredded cheddar cheese
- 1/4 cup cooked bacon, crumbled
- 1/4 tsp garlic powder
- 1/4 tsp onion powder
- 1/2 cup panko breadcrumbs
- 2 tbsp melted butter

Directions:

1. Preheat your Breville Smart Oven Air Fryer Pro to 375°F using the Bake function.
2. In a mixing bowl, combine the cream cheese, cheddar cheese, bacon, garlic powder, and onion powder until smooth.
3. Stuff each jalapeño half with the cream cheese mixture.
4. In a separate bowl, mix the panko breadcrumbs with the melted butter.
5. Press the breadcrumb mixture onto the top of each stuffed jalapeño.
6. Place the jalapeño poppers in the air fryer basket in a single layer.
7. Bake for 12-15 minutes, or until the poppers are golden and the cheese is melted.

Tip: For a milder version, use mini bell peppers instead of jalapeños.

Sweet Potato Chips

Prep: 10 Minutes | Cook: 15 Minutes | Makes: 4 Servings

Ingredients:
- 2 medium sweet potatoes, thinly sliced
- 1 tbsp olive oil
- 1/2 tsp smoked paprika
- 1/2 tsp garlic powder
- Salt to taste

Directions:
1. Preheat your Breville Smart Oven Air Fryer Pro to 350°F using the Air Fry function.
2. In a large bowl, toss the sweet potato slices with olive oil, smoked paprika, garlic powder, and salt.
3. Arrange the sweet potato slices in a single layer in the air fryer basket.
4. Air fry for 12-15 minutes, shaking the basket halfway through, until the chips are crispy and golden.
5. Serve immediately as a snack or alongside your favorite dip.

Tip: To ensure even cooking, try to slice the sweet potatoes as evenly as possible using a mandoline.

Coconut Shrimp

Prep: 15 Minutes | Cook: 10 Minutes | Makes: 4 Servings

Ingredients:
- 1 lb large shrimp, peeled and deveined
- 1/2 cup all-purpose flour
- 2 large eggs, beaten
- 1 cup shredded coconut (sweetened or unsweetened)
- 1/2 cup panko breadcrumbs
- 1/2 tsp garlic powder
- 1/2 tsp paprika
- Salt and pepper to taste
- Sweet chili sauce for dipping

Directions:
1. Preheat your Breville Smart Oven Air Fryer Pro to 400°F using the Air Fry function.
2. In a shallow dish, combine the flour, garlic powder, paprika, salt, and pepper.
3. In another dish, place the beaten eggs.
4. In a third dish, mix together the shredded coconut and panko breadcrumbs.
5. Dredge each shrimp in the flour mixture, then dip into the beaten eggs, and finally coat with the coconut-panko mixture.
6. Place the coated shrimp in the air fryer basket in a single layer.
7. Air fry for 8-10 minutes, flipping halfway through, until the shrimp are golden and crispy.
8. Serve immediately with sweet chili sauce for dipping.

Tip: For extra crunch, lightly spray the shrimp with cooking spray before air frying.

FETA AND TOMATO DIP
Prep: 5 Minutes | Cook: 20 Minutes | Makes: 4 Servings

Ingredients:
- 1 block (8 oz) feta cheese
- 1 pint cherry tomatoes
- 3 cloves garlic, minced
- 2 tbsp olive oil
- 1 tsp dried oregano
- Salt and pepper to taste
- Fresh basil for garnish
- Toasted bread or crackers for serving

Directions:
1. Preheat your Breville Smart Oven Air Fryer Pro to 375°F using the Bake function.
2. Place the feta cheese in the center of a baking dish. Scatter the cherry tomatoes around the feta.
3. Drizzle the olive oil over the feta and tomatoes. Sprinkle with minced garlic, oregano, salt, and pepper.
4. Bake for 20 minutes, or until the tomatoes are blistered and the feta is soft.
5. Garnish with fresh basil and serve immediately with toasted bread or crackers.

Tip: For a touch of heat, add a pinch of red pepper flakes before baking.

STUFFED MUSHROOMS
Prep: 15 Minutes | Cook: 12 Minutes | Makes: 4 Servings

Ingredients:
- 12 large cremini or white mushrooms, stems removed
- 4 oz cream cheese, softened
- 1/4 cup grated Parmesan cheese
- 1/4 cup cooked bacon, crumbled
- 1/4 cup breadcrumbs
- 2 tbsp chopped fresh parsley
- 1 clove garlic, minced
- Salt and pepper to taste

Directions:
1. Preheat your Breville Smart Oven Air Fryer Pro to 375°F using the Air Fry function.
2. In a mixing bowl, combine the cream cheese, Parmesan cheese, bacon, breadcrumbs, parsley, garlic, salt, and pepper.
3. Stuff each mushroom cap with the cream cheese mixture, pressing down gently to fill.
4. Arrange the stuffed mushrooms in the air fryer basket.
5. Air fry for 10-12 minutes, or until the mushrooms are tender and the tops are golden.
6. Serve warm.

Tip: For a vegetarian version, omit the bacon and add finely chopped spinach or artichokes to the filling.

Goat Cheese Crostini

Prep: 10 Minutes | Cook: 10 Minutes | Makes: 4 Servings

Ingredients:

- 1 baguette, sliced into 1/2-inch rounds
- 4 oz goat cheese
- 1/4 cup honey
- 1/4 cup chopped walnuts
- 1 tsp fresh thyme leaves
- Olive oil for brushing

Directions:

1. Preheat your Breville Smart Oven Air Fryer Pro to 375°F using the Bake function.
2. Brush each baguette slice with olive oil on both sides and arrange them on a baking sheet.
3. Bake for 5 minutes, or until lightly toasted.
4. Spread a generous layer of goat cheese on each toasted baguette slice.
5. Drizzle with honey and sprinkle with chopped walnuts and fresh thyme.
6. Return to the oven and bake for an additional 5 minutes, or until the goat cheese is warm.
7. Serve immediately.

Tip: You can add a slice of fresh fig or pear on top of the goat cheese for an extra burst of flavor.

Avocado Fries

Prep: 10 Minutes | Cook: 8 Minutes | Makes: 4 Servings

Ingredients:

- 2 ripe avocados, peeled and sliced into wedges
- 1/2 cup all-purpose flour
- 2 large eggs, beaten
- 1 cup panko breadcrumbs
- 1/4 cup grated Parmesan cheese
- 1 tsp smoked paprika
- Salt and pepper to taste
- Ranch dressing or aioli for dipping

Directions:

1. Preheat your Breville Smart Oven Air Fryer Pro to 400°F using the Air Fry function.
2. In a shallow dish, place the flour. In another dish, place the beaten eggs. In a third dish, combine the panko breadcrumbs, Parmesan cheese, smoked paprika, salt, and pepper.
3. Coat each avocado wedge in flour, then dip in the beaten eggs, and finally coat with the breadcrumb mixture.
4. Place the avocado wedges in the air fryer basket in a single layer.
5. Air fry for 6-8 minutes, flipping halfway through, until the avocado fries are golden and crispy.
6. Serve immediately with ranch dressing or aioli for dipping.

Tip: For a gluten-free option, use almond flour and gluten-free breadcrumbs.

Brie Bites with Cranberry Sauce

Prep: 10 Minutes | Cook: 8 Minutes | Makes: 4 Servings

Ingredients:
- 1 sheet puff pastry, thawed
- 8 oz Brie cheese, cut into small cubes
- 1/2 cup cranberry sauce (store-bought or homemade)
- 1 egg, beaten (for egg wash)
- Fresh thyme leaves for garnish (optional)

Directions:
1. Preheat your Breville Smart Oven Air Fryer Pro to 375°F using the Air Fry function.
2. Roll out the puff pastry sheet on a floured surface and cut it into 12 equal squares.
3. Place a cube of Brie cheese in the center of each square and top with a small spoonful of cranberry sauce.
4. Fold the corners of the pastry over the filling to form a bundle, pinching the edges to seal.
5. Brush the tops of the Brie bites with the beaten egg.
6. Place the bites in the air fryer basket and air fry for 6-8 minutes, or until the pastry is golden and puffed.
7. Garnish with fresh thyme leaves if desired, and serve warm.

Tip: For a savory twist, try using fig jam or apricot preserves instead of cranberry sauce.

Caprese Stuffed Portobello Mushrooms

Prep: 10 Minutes | Cook: 15 Minutes | Makes: 4 Servings

Ingredients:
- 4 large portobello mushrooms, stems removed
- 1 cup cherry tomatoes, halved
- 8 oz fresh mozzarella, sliced
- 2 tbsp pesto sauce
- Fresh basil leaves for garnish
- Balsamic glaze for drizzling
- Olive oil for brushing
- Salt and pepper to taste

Directions:
1. Preheat your Breville Smart Oven Air Fryer Pro to 375°F using the Bake function.
2. Brush the mushroom caps with olive oil and season with salt and pepper.
3. Place the mushrooms in a baking dish, gill-side up.
4. Spread a thin layer of pesto sauce inside each mushroom cap.
5. Top with cherry tomatoes and mozzarella slices.
6. Bake for 12-15 minutes, or until the mushrooms are tender and the cheese is melted and bubbly.
7. Garnish with fresh basil leaves and drizzle with balsamic glaze before serving.

Tip: For added flavor, sprinkle some grated Parmesan cheese over the mozzarella before baking.

Bacon-Wrapped Jalapeño Shrimp

Prep: 15 Minutes | Cook: 10 Minutes | Makes: 4 Servings

Ingredients:
- 12 large shrimp, peeled and deveined
- 6 slices of bacon, halved
- 1/4 cup cream cheese, softened
- 1 jalapeño, seeded and finely diced
- 1/2 tsp garlic powder
- Toothpicks

Directions:
1. Preheat your Breville Smart Oven Air Fryer Pro to 400°F using the Air Fry function.
2. In a small bowl, mix the cream cheese, diced jalapeño, and garlic powder.
3. Cut a small slit down the back of each shrimp to create a pocket.
4. Fill each pocket with a small amount of the cream cheese mixture.
5. Wrap each shrimp with a half-slice of bacon and secure with a toothpick.
6. Place the shrimp in the air fryer basket in a single layer.
7. Air fry for 8-10 minutes, or until the bacon is crispy and the shrimp are cooked through.
8. Serve immediately.

Tip: For a milder version, use mini sweet peppers instead of jalapeños in the filling.

Spinach and Feta Stuffed Phyllo Cups

Prep: 15 Minutes | Cook: 12 Minutes | Makes: 4 Servings

Ingredients:
- 1 package phyllo pastry cups
- 1 cup fresh spinach, chopped
- 1/2 cup crumbled feta cheese
- 1/4 cup cream cheese, softened
- 1 clove garlic, minced
- 1/4 tsp ground nutmeg
- Salt and pepper to taste
- Olive oil for brushing

Directions:
1. Preheat your Breville Smart Oven Air Fryer Pro to 350°F using the Bake function.
2. In a bowl, mix together the chopped spinach, feta cheese, cream cheese, garlic, nutmeg, salt, and pepper.
3. Spoon the spinach mixture into each phyllo cup, filling them generously.
4. Place the filled phyllo cups on a baking sheet.
5. Bake for 10-12 minutes, or until the filling is heated through and the phyllo cups are golden and crisp.
6. Serve warm.

Tip: For added crunch, sprinkle the tops with toasted pine nuts before baking.

Chickpea Falafel Bites

Prep: 15 Minutes | Cook: 15 Minutes | Makes: 4 Servings

Ingredients:

- 1 can (15 oz) chickpeas, drained and rinsed
- 1/4 cup chopped fresh parsley
- 1/4 cup chopped onion
- 2 cloves garlic, minced
- 1 tbsp ground cumin
- 1 tsp ground coriander
- 1/4 tsp cayenne pepper
- 2 tbsp all-purpose flour
- 1/2 tsp baking powder
- Salt and pepper to taste
- Olive oil spray
- Tzatziki or hummus for serving

Directions:

1. Preheat your Breville Smart Oven Air Fryer Pro to 375°F using the Air Fry function.
2. In a food processor, combine the chickpeas, parsley, onion, garlic, cumin, coriander, cayenne pepper, flour, baking powder, salt, and pepper. Pulse until the mixture is well combined but still slightly chunky.
3. Form the mixture into small balls or patties.
4. Lightly spray the falafel bites with olive oil spray.
5. Place the falafel bites in the air fryer basket in a single layer.
6. Air fry for 12-15 minutes, turning halfway through, until the falafel is golden and crispy.
7. Serve warm with tzatziki or hummus for dipping.

Tip: Serve falafel bites in pita bread with fresh veggies for a heartier snack.

Stuffed Mini Bell Peppers

Prep: 15 Minutes | Cook: 10 Minutes | Makes: 4 Servings

Ingredients:

- 12 mini bell peppers, tops cut off and seeds removed
- 4 oz cream cheese, softened
- 1/4 cup shredded cheddar cheese
- 1/4 cup cooked bacon, crumbled
- 1 tbsp chopped chives
- 1/2 tsp garlic powder
- Salt and pepper to taste

Directions:

1. Preheat your Breville Smart Oven Air Fryer Pro to 375°F using the Air Fry function.
2. In a mixing bowl, combine the cream cheese, cheddar cheese, bacon, chives, garlic powder, salt, and pepper until well blended.
3. Stuff each mini bell pepper with the cheese mixture, pressing it in tightly.
4. Place the stuffed peppers in the air fryer basket in a single layer.
5. Air fry for 8-10 minutes, or until the peppers are tender and the cheese is melted and bubbly.

Tip: Replace bacon with sun-dried tomatoes or spinach for a vegetarian twist.

Goat Cheese and Honey Stuffed Dates

Prep: 10 Minutes | Cook: 8 Minutes | Makes: 4 Servings

Ingredients:

- 12 Medjool dates, pitted
- 4 oz goat cheese, softened
- 1/4 cup chopped walnuts
- 2 tbsp honey
- Fresh thyme leaves for garnish (optional)

Directions:

1. Preheat your Breville Smart Oven Air Fryer Pro to 350°F using the Bake function.
2. Carefully open each date and stuff with about 1 teaspoon of goat cheese.
3. Place the stuffed dates in a baking dish.
4. Sprinkle chopped walnuts over the dates and drizzle with honey.
5. Bake for 8-10 minutes, or until the dates are warmed through and the cheese is soft.
6. Garnish with fresh thyme leaves if desired and serve warm.

Tip: You can also wrap each date with a half slice of prosciutto before baking for an added savory element.

Parmesan Truffle Potato Wedges

Prep: 10 Minutes | Cook: 20 Minutes | Makes: 4 Servings

Ingredients:

- 4 medium russet potatoes, cut into wedges
- 2 tbsp olive oil
- 1/2 cup grated Parmesan cheese
- 1 tsp garlic powder
- Salt and pepper to taste
- 1 tbsp truffle oil
- Fresh parsley for garnish

Directions:

1. Preheat your Breville Smart Oven Air Fryer Pro to 400°F using the Air Fry function.
2. In a large bowl, toss the potato wedges with olive oil, Parmesan cheese, garlic powder, salt, and pepper until well coated.
3. Arrange the potato wedges in the air fryer basket in a single layer.
4. Air fry for 18-20 minutes, shaking the basket halfway through, until the wedges are crispy and golden.
5. Drizzle the hot potato wedges with truffle oil and garnish with fresh parsley before serving.

Tip: For extra flavor, sprinkle the wedges with a bit of smoked paprika or chili powder before air frying.

Spinach Artichoke Stuffed Crescent Rolls

Prep: 15 Minutes | Cook: 12 Minutes | Makes: 4 Servings

Ingredients:

- 1 can refrigerated crescent roll dough
- 1/2 cup frozen spinach, thawed and drained
- 1/2 cup canned artichoke hearts, chopped
- 1/4 cup cream cheese, softened
- 1/4 cup shredded mozzarella cheese
- 1/4 tsp garlic powder
- Salt and pepper to taste

Directions:

1. Preheat your Breville Smart Oven Air Fryer Pro to 375°F using the Bake function.

2. In a mixing bowl, combine the spinach, artichoke hearts, cream cheese, mozzarella cheese, garlic powder, salt, and pepper.

3. Unroll the crescent roll dough and separate into triangles.

4. Place a spoonful of the spinach and artichoke mixture onto the wide end of each triangle.

5. Roll up the dough, starting from the wide end, and place on a baking sheet.

6. Bake for 10-12 minutes, or until the crescent rolls are golden and cooked through.

7. Serve warm.

Tip: These crescent rolls can be made ahead and reheated in the air fryer for a quick snack.

Mozzarella Stuffed Meatballs

Prep: 20 Minutes | Cook: 12 Minutes | Makes: 4 Servings

Ingredients:

- 1 lb ground beef or turkey
- 1/4 cup breadcrumbs
- 1/4 cup grated Parmesan cheese
- 1 large egg
- 2 cloves garlic, minced
- 1 tsp Italian seasoning
- Salt and pepper to taste
- 8 small mozzarella balls (bocconcini)
- Marinara sauce for serving

Directions:

1. Preheat your Breville Smart Oven Air Fryer Pro to 375°F using the Air Fry function.

2. In a large bowl, combine the ground meat, breadcrumbs, Parmesan cheese, egg, garlic, Italian seasoning, salt, and pepper. Mix until well combined.

3. Divide the meat mixture into 8 equal portions. Flatten each portion slightly and place a mozzarella ball in the center. Wrap the meat around the cheese, forming a sealed meatball.

4. Place the meatballs in the air fryer basket in a single layer.

5. Air fry for 10-12 minutes, or until the meatballs are cooked through and golden brown.

6. Serve with marinara sauce for dipping.

Tip: For extra flavor, you can add a small piece of fresh basil or a sun-dried tomato inside each meatball with the mozzarella.

Spicy Sriracha Cauliflower Bites

Prep: 10 Minutes | Cook: 15 Minutes | Makes: 4 Servings

Ingredients:

- 1 small cauliflower (florets)
- 1/2 cup flour
- 1/2 cup water
- 1/4 cup Sriracha
- 2 tbsp honey
- 1 tbsp soy sauce
- 1/2 tsp garlic powder
- 1/2 tsp smoked paprika
- Salt, pepper, green onions, sesame seeds

Directions:

1. Preheat the Breville Air Fryer to 375°F.
2. Mix flour, water, garlic powder, paprika, salt, and pepper for batter. Coat cauliflower.
3. Air fry for 12-15 minutes, shaking halfway.
4. Combine Sriracha, honey, and soy sauce. Toss with cauliflower.
5. Garnish with green onions and sesame seeds.

Tip: Adjust the level of spiciness by adding more or less Sriracha sauce according to your preference.

Cheesy Jalapeño Cornbread Muffins

Prep: 10 Minutes | Cook: 15 Minutes | Makes: 12 Muffins

Ingredients:

- 1 cup cornmeal
- 1 cup all-purpose flour
- 1/4 cup sugar
- 1 tbsp baking powder
- 1/2 tsp salt
- 1 cup milk
- 1/3 cup vegetable oil
- 1 large egg
- 1/2 cup shredded cheddar cheese
- 1/4 cup diced jalapeños (seeded for less heat)
- 1/4 cup corn kernels (fresh or canned)

Directions:

1. Preheat Breville Air Fryer Pro to 375°F (Bake).
2. Mix cornmeal, flour, sugar, baking powder, and salt in a bowl.
3. In another bowl, combine milk, oil, and egg.
4. Add wet ingredients to dry and mix. Fold in cheese, jalapeños, and corn.
5. Grease a muffin tin and fill cups 3/4 full.
6. Bake for 12-15 minutes until golden and a toothpick comes out clean.

Tip: For an extra cheesy twist, sprinkle a little more cheddar cheese on top of each muffin before baking.

Teriyaki Chicken Skewers

Prep: 15 Minutes (Plus Marinating Time) | Cook: 10 Minutes | Makes: 4 Servings

Ingredients:

- 1 lb chicken breast, cut into bite-sized pieces
- 1/4 cup soy sauce
- 2 tbsp honey
- 2 tbsp rice vinegar
- 1 tbsp sesame oil
- 2 cloves garlic, minced
- 1 tbsp grated ginger
- 1/4 cup pineapple juice
- 1 tbsp cornstarch (optional, for thicker sauce)
- Bamboo skewers, soaked in water for 30 minutes
- Sesame seeds and chopped green onions for garnish

Directions:

1. In a bowl, mix together the soy sauce, honey, rice vinegar, sesame oil, garlic, ginger, and pineapple juice to make the marinade.

2. Add the chicken pieces to the marinade and let them marinate in the refrigerator for at least 30 minutes, or up to 2 hours.

3. Preheat your Breville Smart Oven Air Fryer Pro to 375°F using the Air Fry function.

4. Thread the marinated chicken pieces onto the soaked bamboo skewers.

5. Place the skewers in the air fryer basket in a single layer.

6. Air fry for 8-10 minutes, turning halfway through, until the chicken is cooked through and slightly charred.

7. Garnish with sesame seeds and chopped green onions before serving.

Tip: For a thicker teriyaki glaze, simmer the remaining marinade with cornstarch until thickened and brush it over the chicken before serving.

Sweet Potato and Black Bean Quesadillas

Prep: 15 Minutes | Cook: 10 Minutes | Makes: 4 Servings

Ingredients:

- 2 medium sweet potatoes, peeled and diced
- 1 can (15 oz) black beans, drained and rinsed
- 1/2 cup shredded Monterey Jack cheese
- 1/2 cup diced red onion
- 1 tsp cumin
- 1/2 tsp smoked paprika
- Salt and pepper to taste
- 4 large flour tortillas
- Olive oil for brushing
- Salsa and sour cream for serving

Directions:

1. Preheat your Breville Smart Oven Air Fryer Pro to 375°F using the Bake function.
2. In a large mixing bowl, toss the diced sweet potatoes with olive oil, cumin, smoked paprika, salt, and pepper.
3. Spread the sweet potatoes on a baking sheet and bake for 15-20 minutes, or until tender.
4. In a separate bowl, mix the roasted sweet potatoes with black beans, diced onion, and shredded cheese.
5. Place a tortilla on a flat surface and spread the sweet potato mixture over half of the tortilla. Fold the other half over to form a quesadilla.
6. Brush both sides of the quesadilla with a little olive oil and place in the air fryer basket.
7. Air fry for 5-7 minutes, flipping halfway through, until the tortilla is crispy and the cheese is melted.
8. Cut into wedges and serve with salsa and sour cream.

Tip: For added flavor, add a spoonful of guacamole inside the quesadilla before folding.

Coconut-Crusted Avocado Fries

Prep: 10 Minutes | Cook: 8 Minutes | Makes: 4 Servings

Ingredients:

- 2 ripe avocados, peeled and sliced into wedges
- 1/2 cup all-purpose flour
- 2 large eggs, beaten
- 1/2 cup panko breadcrumbs
- 1/2 cup shredded coconut (sweetened or unsweetened)
- 1/2 tsp garlic powder
- Salt and pepper to taste
- Lime wedges and sweet chili sauce for serving

Directions:

1. Preheat your Breville Smart Oven Air Fryer Pro to 400°F using the Air Fry function.
2. In a shallow dish, place the flour. In another dish, place the beaten eggs. In a third dish, combine the panko breadcrumbs, shredded coconut, garlic powder, salt, and pepper.
3. Coat each avocado wedge in flour, then dip in the beaten eggs, and finally coat with the coconut-panko mixture.
4. Place the coated avocado wedges in the air fryer basket in a single layer.
5. Air fry for 6-8 minutes, flipping halfway through, until the avocado fries are golden and crispy.
6. Serve with lime wedges and sweet chili sauce for dipping.

Tip: For a zesty kick, sprinkle the avocado fries with a little lime zest before serving.

CHAPTER 3: MAIN COURSES

LEMON HERB CHICKEN

Ingredients:

- 4 boneless, skinless chicken breasts
- 2 tbsp olive oil
- 2 tbsp lemon juice
- 2 cloves garlic, minced
- 1 tsp dried oregano
- 1 tsp dried thyme
- Salt and pepper to taste
- 1 lb baby potatoes, halved
- 1 cup baby carrots
- 1 cup broccoli florets

Directions:

1. Preheat your Breville Smart Oven Air Fryer Pro to 375°F using the Air Fry function.

2. In a small bowl, mix together the olive oil, lemon juice, garlic, oregano, thyme, salt, and pepper.

3. Brush the chicken breasts with the lemon herb mixture and let them marinate for 10 minutes.

4. In a separate bowl, toss the baby potatoes, carrots, and broccoli with a little olive oil, salt, and pepper.

5. Arrange the marinated chicken breasts in the air fryer basket, with the vegetables spread around them.

6. Air fry for 20-25 minutes, turning the chicken and vegetables halfway through, until the chicken is cooked through and the vegetables are tender.

7. Serve hot with a squeeze of fresh lemon juice.

Tip: For added flavor, garnish the chicken with fresh parsley or dill before serving.

STUFFED BELL PEPPERS WITH GROUND TURKEY

Prep: 20 Minutes | Cook: 30 Minutes | Makes: 4 Servings

Ingredients:

- 4 large bell peppers, tops cut off and seeds removed
- 1/2 lb ground turkey
- 1 cup cooked quinoa
- 1 small onion, diced
- 1 can (15 oz) diced tomatoes, drained
- 1/2 cup shredded mozzarella cheese
- 1 tsp ground cumin
- 1/2 tsp smoked paprika
- Salt and pepper to taste
- Fresh parsley for garnish

Directions:

1. Preheat your Breville Smart Oven Air Fryer Pro to 375°F using the Bake function.

2. In a skillet, cook the ground turkey and diced onion over medium heat until the turkey is browned and the onion is soft.

3. Stir in the cooked quinoa, diced tomatoes, cumin, smoked paprika, salt, and pepper. Cook for another 2-3 minutes.

4. Stuff each bell pepper with the turkey-quinoa mixture, pressing it down gently.

5. Place the stuffed peppers in a baking dish and top each with shredded mozzarella cheese.
6. Bake for 25-30 minutes, or until the peppers are tender and the cheese is melted and golden.
7. Garnish with fresh parsley before serving.

Tip: For a vegetarian option, substitute the ground turkey with black beans or lentils.

SALMON WITH HONEY SOY GLAZE
Prep: 10 Minutes | Cook: 12 Minutes | Makes: 4 Servings

Ingredients:

- 4 salmon fillets
- 2 tbsp soy sauce
- 2 tbsp honey
- 1 tbsp rice vinegar
- 1 tbsp sesame oil
- 2 cloves garlic, minced
- 1 tsp grated ginger
- Sesame seeds and chopped green onions for garnish

Directions:

1. Preheat your Breville Smart Oven Air Fryer Pro to 400°F using the Air Fry function.
2. In a small bowl, whisk together the soy sauce, honey, rice vinegar, sesame oil, garlic, and ginger to make the glaze.
3. Brush the salmon fillets generously with the glaze and let them marinate for 10 minutes.
4. Place the salmon fillets in the air fryer basket, skin-side down.
5. Air fry for 10-12 minutes, or until the salmon is cooked through and slightly caramelized on top.
6. Garnish with sesame seeds and chopped green onions before serving.

Tip: Serve the salmon with steamed rice and sautéed greens for a complete meal.

PORK CHOPS WITH APPLE CIDER GLAZE
Prep: 15 Minutes | Cook: 20 Minutes | Makes: 4 Servings

Ingredients:
- 4 bone-in pork chops
- 1/4 cup apple cider
- 2 tbsp Dijon mustard
- 2 tbsp honey
- 1 tbsp apple cider vinegar
- 1 tsp garlic powder
- 1 tsp dried thyme
- Salt and pepper to taste
- Fresh thyme for garnish

Directions:

1. Preheat your Breville Smart Oven Air Fryer Pro to 375°F using the Air Fry function.

2. In a small bowl, mix together the apple cider, Dijon mustard, honey, apple cider vinegar, garlic powder, dried thyme, salt, and pepper to make the glaze.

3. Brush the pork chops with the glaze and let them marinate for 10 minutes.

4. Place the pork chops in the air fryer basket in a single layer.

5. Air fry for 15-20 minutes, turning halfway through, until the pork chops are cooked through and caramelized on the edges.

6. Garnish with fresh thyme before serving.

Tip: Serve these pork chops with roasted sweet potatoes and a simple green salad for a well-rounded meal.

CRISPY TOFU STIR-FRY

Prep: 15 Minutes | Cook: 20 Minutes | Makes: 4 Servings

Ingredients:

- 1 block (14 oz) firm tofu, drained and cubed
- 2 tbsp cornstarch
- 2 tbsp soy sauce
- 1 tbsp sesame oil
- 1 tbsp rice vinegar
- 1 tbsp honey or maple syrup
- 2 cloves garlic, minced
- 1 tsp grated ginger
- 1 red bell pepper, sliced
- 1 cup broccoli florets
- 1 carrot, julienned
- 1/2 cup snap peas
- Cooked jasmine rice for serving
- Sesame seeds and chopped green onions for garnish

Directions:

1. Preheat your Breville Smart Oven Air Fryer Pro to 375°F using the Air Fry function.

2. Toss the cubed tofu with cornstarch until evenly coated. Place the tofu in the air fryer basket in a single layer.

3. Air fry the tofu for 15-18 minutes, shaking the basket halfway through, until the tofu is crispy and golden.

4. In a small bowl, whisk together the soy sauce, sesame oil, rice vinegar, honey, garlic, and ginger to make the stir-fry sauce.

5. In a large skillet, heat a little sesame oil over medium heat. Add the bell pepper, broccoli, carrot, and snap peas, and stir-fry for 3-4 minutes until the vegetables are tender-crisp.

6. Add the crispy tofu to the skillet and pour the stir-fry sauce over the top. Toss everything together until well coated and heated through.

7. Serve the stir-fry over jasmine rice and garnish with sesame seeds and chopped green onions.

Tip: For extra flavor, add a splash of chili garlic sauce to the stir-fry sauce for a bit of heat.

Chicken Parmesan with Marinara

Prep: 20 Minutes | Cook: 25 Minutes | Makes: 4 Servings

Ingredients:

- 4 boneless, skinless chicken breasts
- 1 cup all-purpose flour
- 2 large eggs, beaten
- 1 1/2 cups panko breadcrumbs
- 1/2 cup grated Parmesan cheese
- 1 tsp dried oregano
- 1 tsp garlic powder
- Salt and pepper to taste
- 2 cups marinara sauce
- 1 1/2 cups shredded mozzarella cheese
- Fresh basil for garnish

Directions:

1. Preheat your Breville Smart Oven Air Fryer Pro to 375°F using the Bake function.

2. Set up a breading station with three shallow dishes: one with flour, one with beaten eggs, and one with panko breadcrumbs mixed with Parmesan cheese, oregano, garlic powder, salt, and pepper.

3. Dip each chicken breast first in the flour, then in the eggs, and finally coat with the breadcrumb mixture.

4. Place the breaded chicken breasts on a baking sheet and bake for 20-25 minutes, or until the chicken is golden and cooked through.

5. Spread a thin layer of marinara sauce in a baking dish. Place the baked chicken breasts on top and spoon more marinara sauce over each.

6. Sprinkle shredded mozzarella cheese over the chicken and bake for an additional 5-7 minutes, or until the cheese is melted and bubbly.

7. Garnish with fresh basil before serving.

Tip: Serve with a side of spaghetti or a fresh green salad for a complete Italian-inspired meal.

Pork Tenderloin with Garlic Herb Rub

Prep: 15 Minutes | Cook: 25 Minutes | Makes: 4 Servings

Ingredients:

- 1 1/2 lbs pork tenderloin
- 2 tbsp olive oil
- 4 cloves garlic, minced
- 1 tsp dried rosemary
- 1 tsp dried thyme
- 1 tsp smoked paprika
- 1/2 tsp salt
- 1/2 tsp black pepper
- Fresh parsley for garnish

Directions:

1. Preheat your Breville Smart Oven Air Fryer Pro to 375°F using the Air Fry function.

2. In a small bowl, mix together the olive oil, minced garlic, rosemary, thyme, smoked paprika, salt, and pepper to create a rub.

3. Rub the garlic herb mixture all over the pork tenderloin, ensuring it's evenly coated.

4. Place the pork tenderloin in the air fryer basket.

5. Air fry for 20-25 minutes, turning halfway through, until the pork reaches an internal temperature of 145°F and is golden brown on the outside.

6. Let the pork rest for 5 minutes before slicing.

7. Garnish with fresh parsley and serve.

Tip: Pair the pork tenderloin with roasted vegetables or mashed potatoes for a hearty dinner.

Ratatouille with Balsamic Glaze

Prep: 20 Minutes | Cook: 30 Minutes | Makes: 4 Servings

Ingredients:

- 1 small eggplant, thinly sliced
- 1 zucchini, thinly sliced
- 1 yellow squash, thinly sliced
- 1 red bell pepper, thinly sliced
- 1 small red onion, thinly sliced
- 2 tomatoes, thinly sliced
- 2 cloves garlic, minced
- 2 tbsp olive oil
- 1 tsp dried thyme
- 1 tsp dried basil
- Salt and pepper to taste
- Balsamic glaze for drizzling
- Fresh basil for garnish

Directions:

1. Preheat your Breville Smart Oven Air Fryer Pro to 375°F using the Bake function.

2. In a baking dish, arrange the sliced vegetables in alternating layers (e.g., eggplant, zucchini, squash, bell pepper, onion, tomato) in a circular pattern, slightly overlapping each slice.

3. Drizzle the minced garlic and olive oil over the vegetables and season with thyme, basil, salt, and pepper.

4. Cover the dish with foil and bake for 25-30 minutes, or until the vegetables are tender.

5. Remove the foil and bake for an additional 5 minutes to allow the vegetables to brown slightly.

6. Drizzle with balsamic glaze and garnish with fresh basil before serving.

Tip: Serve this ratatouille as a main course with crusty bread or as a side dish alongside grilled meats.

Cajun Shrimp and Sausage Skewers

Prep: 15 Minutes | Cook: 10 Minutes | Makes: 4 Servings

Ingredients:

- 1 lb large shrimp, peeled and deveined
- 8 oz andouille sausage, sliced into rounds
- 1 red bell pepper, cut into squares
- 1 green bell pepper, cut into squares
- 1 red onion, cut into squares
- 2 tbsp olive oil
- 2 tbsp Cajun seasoning
- Juice of 1 lemon
- Bamboo skewers, soaked in water for 30 minutes
- Fresh parsley for garnish

Directions:

1. Preheat your Breville Smart Oven Air Fryer Pro to 400°F using the Air Fry function.
2. In a large bowl, toss the shrimp, sausage, bell peppers, and onion with olive oil, Cajun seasoning, and lemon juice until well coated.
3. Thread the shrimp, sausage, and vegetables onto the soaked bamboo skewers, alternating the ingredients.
4. Place the skewers in the air fryer basket in a single layer.
5. Air fry for 8-10 minutes, turning halfway through, until the shrimp are cooked through and the sausage is slightly charred.
6. Garnish with fresh parsley before serving.

Tip: Serve these skewers over rice or with a side of cornbread for a complete meal.

Mediterranean Chicken with Olives

Prep: 15 Minutes | Cook: 25 Minutes | Makes: 4 Servings

Ingredients:

- 4 boneless, skinless chicken thighs
- 1/4 cup olive oil
- 2 tbsp lemon juice
- 3 cloves garlic, minced
- 1 tsp dried oregano
- 1/2 tsp smoked paprika
- Salt and pepper to taste
- 1/2 cup Kalamata olives, pitted and halved
- 1/2 cup cherry tomatoes, halved
- 1/4 cup crumbled feta cheese
- Fresh parsley for garnish

Directions:

1. Preheat your Breville Smart Oven Air Fryer Pro to 375°F using the Air Fry function.
2. In a small bowl, whisk together the olive oil, lemon juice, garlic, oregano, smoked paprika, salt, and pepper.

3. Toss the chicken thighs in the marinade, ensuring they are well coated. Let them marinate for 10 minutes.

4. Place the chicken thighs in the air fryer basket, skin-side up.

5. Air fry for 20-25 minutes, turning halfway through, until the chicken is cooked through and golden brown.

6. In the last 5 minutes of cooking, add the olives and cherry tomatoes to the air fryer basket to warm them through.

7. Remove the chicken and vegetables from the air fryer and sprinkle with crumbled feta cheese.

8. Garnish with fresh parsley before serving.

Tip: Serve this dish with a side of couscous or a simple Greek salad.

Beef and Mushroom Stroganoff

Prep: 15 Minutes | Cook: 30 Minutes | Makes: 4 Servings

Ingredients:

- 1 lb beef sirloin, sliced into thin strips
- 2 tbsp olive oil
- 1 onion, diced
- 2 cloves garlic, minced
- 8 oz mushrooms, sliced
- 1 cup beef broth
- 1/2 cup sour cream
- 1 tbsp Dijon mustard
- 1 tsp Worcestershire sauce
- 1 tbsp all-purpose flour
- Salt and pepper to taste
- Cooked egg noodles for serving
- Fresh parsley for garnish

Directions:

1. Preheat your Breville Smart Oven Air Fryer Pro to 375°F using the Bake function.

2. Heat olive oil in a skillet over medium heat. Add the beef strips and cook until browned on all sides. Remove from the skillet and set aside.

3. In the same skillet, sauté the onion and garlic until softened. Add the mushrooms and cook until they release their juices and begin to brown.

4. Stir in the flour and cook for 1-2 minutes. Gradually add the beef broth, stirring constantly, until the sauce thickens.

5. Stir in the sour cream, Dijon mustard, Worcestershire sauce, salt, and pepper. Return the beef to the skillet and mix well.

6. Transfer the beef and mushroom mixture to a baking dish and bake for 15-20 minutes, or until the beef is tender and the sauce is bubbling.

7. Serve the stroganoff over cooked egg noodles and garnish with fresh parsley.

Tip: For a lower-carb option, serve the stroganoff over cauliflower rice or zucchini noodles.

BBQ Glazed Meatloaf

Prep: 15 Minutes | Cook: 30 Minutes | Makes: 4 Servings

Ingredients:

- 1 lb ground beef
- 1/2 lb ground pork
- 1/2 cup breadcrumbs
- 1/4 cup grated onion
- 1/4 cup milk
- 1 large egg, beaten
- 2 tbsp ketchup
- 1 tbsp Worcestershire sauce
- 1 tsp garlic powder
- 1 tsp smoked paprika
- Salt and pepper to taste
- 1/2 cup BBQ sauce

Directions:

1. Preheat your Breville Smart Oven Air Fryer Pro to 350°F using the Air Fry function.

2. In a large mixing bowl, combine the ground beef, ground pork, breadcrumbs, grated onion, milk, beaten egg, ketchup, Worcestershire sauce, garlic powder, smoked paprika, salt, and pepper. Mix until well combined.

3. Shape the mixture into a loaf and place it in a loaf pan that fits inside the air fryer basket.

4. Air fry for 25-30 minutes, or until the meatloaf is cooked through and reaches an internal temperature of 160°F.

5. In the last 5 minutes of cooking, brush the top of the meatloaf with BBQ sauce and continue cooking until the glaze is caramelized.

6. Let the meatloaf rest for a few minutes before slicing and serving.

Tip: Serve the meatloaf with mashed potatoes and steamed green beans for a comforting meal.

Lemon Garlic Shrimp and Asparagus

Prep: 10 Minutes | Cook: 15 Minutes | Makes: 4 Servings

Ingredients:

- 1 lb large shrimp, peeled and deveined
- 1 bunch asparagus, trimmed
- 3 tbsp olive oil
- 2 tbsp lemon juice
- 4 cloves garlic, minced
- 1 tsp lemon zest
- 1/2 tsp red pepper flakes (optional)
- Salt and pepper to taste
- Fresh parsley for garnish

Directions:

1. Preheat your Breville Smart Oven Air Fryer Pro to 400°F using the Bake function.
2. In a large mixing bowl, toss the shrimp and asparagus with olive oil, lemon juice, garlic, lemon zest, red pepper flakes (if using), salt, and pepper.
3. Arrange the shrimp and asparagus in a single layer on a baking sheet.
4. Bake for 10-12 minutes, or until the shrimp are pink and opaque and the asparagus is tender-crisp.
5. Garnish with fresh parsley and serve immediately.

Tip: Serve this dish over a bed of quinoa or rice for a complete meal.

CHICKEN AND WAFFLES WITH MAPLE BUTTER
Prep: 20 Minutes | Cook: 20 Minutes | Makes: 4 Servings

Ingredients:

- 4 boneless, skinless chicken thighs
- 1 cup buttermilk
- 1 cup all-purpose flour
- 1 tsp garlic powder
- 1 tsp smoked paprika
- 1/2 tsp cayenne pepper
- Salt and pepper to taste
- Cooking spray
- 4 waffles (store-bought or homemade)
- 1/4 cup butter, softened
- 2 tbsp maple syrup

Directions:

1. Preheat your Breville Smart Oven Air Fryer Pro to 375°F using the Air Fry function.
2. In a bowl, soak the chicken thighs in buttermilk for at least 15 minutes (or overnight for extra tenderness).
3. In a shallow dish, combine the flour, garlic powder, smoked paprika, cayenne pepper, salt, and pepper.
4. Remove the chicken from the buttermilk and dredge each piece in the flour mixture, ensuring an even coating.
5. Place the coated chicken in the air fryer basket and lightly spray with cooking spray.
6. Air fry for 18-20 minutes, turning halfway through, until the chicken is golden brown and cooked through.
7. While the chicken is cooking, prepare the waffles according to package instructions or make your own.
8. In a small bowl, mix the softened butter with maple syrup until well combined.
9. Serve the crispy chicken thighs on top of the waffles and drizzle with maple butter.

Tip: For an extra kick, add a dash of hot sauce to the maple butter or serve it on the side.

Moroccan-Spiced Chicken Thighs

Prep: 15 Minutes | Cook: 20 Minutes | Makes: 4 Servings

Ingredients:

- 4 boneless, skinless chicken thighs
- 2 tbsp olive oil
- 1 tsp ground cumin
- 1 tsp ground coriander
- 1 tsp ground turmeric
- 1/2 tsp ground cinnamon
- 1/2 tsp smoked paprika
- 1/4 tsp cayenne pepper (optional)
- Salt and pepper to taste
- 1/4 cup chopped fresh cilantro
- Lemon wedges for serving

Directions:

1. Preheat your Breville Smart Oven Air Fryer Pro to 375°F using the Air Fry function.
2. In a small bowl, mix together the olive oil, cumin, coriander, turmeric, cinnamon, smoked paprika, cayenne pepper (if using), salt, and pepper to create a spice rub.
3. Rub the spice mixture all over the chicken thighs, making sure they are evenly coated.
4. Place the chicken thighs in the air fryer basket in a single layer.
5. Air fry for 18-20 minutes, turning halfway through, until the chicken is cooked through and the outside is golden and slightly crispy.
6. Garnish with chopped fresh cilantro and serve with lemon wedges.

Tip: Serve these chicken thighs with couscous or a simple salad for a complete meal.

Herb-Crusted Salmon with Asparagus

Prep: 10 Minutes | Cook: 15 Minutes | Makes: 4 Servings

Ingredients:

- 4 salmon fillets
- 1 bunch asparagus, trimmed
- 1/4 cup breadcrumbs
- 1/4 cup grated Parmesan cheese
- 2 tbsp olive oil
- 2 tbsp chopped fresh parsley
- 1 tbsp chopped fresh dill
- 1 tsp lemon zest
- Salt and pepper to taste
- Lemon wedges for serving

Directions:

1. Preheat your Breville Smart Oven Air Fryer Pro to 400°F using the Bake function.
2. In a small bowl, mix together the breadcrumbs, Parmesan cheese, olive oil, parsley, dill, lemon zest, salt, and pepper.

3. Place the salmon fillets on a baking sheet and press the breadcrumb mixture onto the top of each fillet.

4. Arrange the asparagus around the salmon on the baking sheet, drizzle with a little olive oil, and season with salt and pepper.

5. Bake for 12-15 minutes, or until the salmon is cooked through and the crust is golden brown.

6. Serve with lemon wedges.

Tip: For an extra burst of flavor, drizzle the salmon with a little lemon juice before serving.

BEEF KOFTA WITH TZATZIKI

Prep: 20 Minutes | Cook: 10 Minutes | Makes: 4 Servings

Ingredients:

- 1 lb ground beef (or lamb)
- 1 small onion, finely grated
- 2 cloves garlic, minced
- 1/4 cup chopped fresh parsley
- 1 tsp ground cumin
- 1 tsp ground coriander
- 1/2 tsp ground cinnamon
- Salt and pepper to taste
- Bamboo skewers, soaked in water for 30 minutes
- Tzatziki sauce for serving
- Pita bread and fresh vegetables for serving

Directions:

1. Preheat your Breville Smart Oven Air Fryer Pro to 375°F using the Air Fry function.

2. In a large mixing bowl, combine the ground beef, grated onion, garlic, parsley, cumin, coriander, cinnamon, salt, and pepper. Mix until well combined.

3. Divide the mixture into 8 equal portions and shape each portion around a bamboo skewer to form kofta kebabs.

4. Place the kofta kebabs in the air fryer basket in a single layer.

5. Air fry for 8-10 minutes, turning halfway through, until the kofta are browned and cooked through.

6. Serve the kofta with tzatziki sauce, pita bread, and fresh vegetables.

Tip: Add a squeeze of lemon juice over the kofta before serving for a bright, fresh flavor.

Spinach and Ricotta Stuffed Shells

Prep: 20 Minutes | Cook: 30 Minutes | Makes: 4 Servings

Ingredients:

- 12 large pasta shells
- 1 cup ricotta cheese
- 1 cup shredded mozzarella cheese, divided
- 1/2 cup grated Parmesan cheese
- 1 egg, beaten
- 1 clove garlic, minced
- 1 cup cooked spinach, drained and chopped
- 2 cups marinara sauce
- Fresh basil for garnish

Directions:

1. Preheat your Breville Smart Oven Air Fryer Pro to 375°F using the Bake function.
2. Cook the pasta shells according to package instructions until al dente. Drain and set aside.
3. In a large mixing bowl, combine the ricotta cheese, 1/2 cup mozzarella cheese, Parmesan cheese, beaten egg, garlic, and spinach. Mix until well combined.
4. Stuff each pasta shell with the ricotta mixture.
5. Spread a thin layer of marinara sauce in the bottom of a baking dish. Arrange the stuffed shells in the dish and cover with the remaining marinara sauce.
6. Sprinkle the remaining 1/2 cup mozzarella cheese over the top.
7. Bake for 25-30 minutes, or until the shells are heated through and the cheese is melted and bubbly.
8. Garnish with fresh basil before serving.

Tip: Serve these stuffed shells with a side of garlic bread or a green salad for a satisfying meal.

Pork Schnitzel with Lemon Caper Sauce

Prep: 20 Minutes | Cook: 15 Minutes | Makes: 4 Servings

Ingredients:

- 4 boneless pork chops, pounded to 1/4-inch thickness
- 1/2 cup all-purpose flour
- 2 large eggs, beaten
- 1 cup panko breadcrumbs
- 1/2 tsp garlic powder
- 1/2 tsp smoked paprika
- Salt and pepper to taste
- Cooking spray
- 2 tbsp butter
- 2 tbsp capers, drained
- Juice of 1 lemon
- Fresh parsley for garnish

Directions:

1. Preheat your Breville Smart Oven Air Fryer Pro to 375°F using the Air Fry function.

2. Set up a breading station with three shallow dishes: one with flour, one with beaten eggs, and one with panko breadcrumbs mixed with garlic powder, smoked paprika, salt, and pepper.

3. Dredge each pork chop in flour, dip in the beaten eggs, and coat with the breadcrumb mixture.

4. Place the breaded pork chops in the air fryer basket and lightly spray with cooking spray.

5. Air fry for 12-15 minutes, turning halfway through, until the pork is golden and crispy.

6. While the pork is cooking, melt the butter in a small skillet over medium heat. Add the capers and lemon juice, and cook for 2-3 minutes until the sauce is warmed through.

7. Serve the schnitzel with the lemon caper sauce drizzled over the top and garnish with fresh parsley.

Tip: Serve this schnitzel with mashed potatoes and a simple cucumber salad for a complete meal.

PESTO-CRUSTED SALMON

Prep: 10 Minutes | Cook: 12 Minutes | Makes: 4 Servings

Ingredients:
- 4 salmon fillets
- 1/4 cup pesto sauce (store-bought or homemade)
- 1/4 cup panko breadcrumbs
- 1/4 cup grated Parmesan cheese
- 1 tbsp olive oil
- Salt and pepper to taste
- Lemon wedges for serving

Directions:
1. Preheat your Breville Smart Oven Air Fryer Pro to 400°F using the Air Fry function.
2. In a small bowl, mix together the panko breadcrumbs, Parmesan cheese, and olive oil.
3. Season the salmon fillets with salt and pepper, then spread a thin layer of pesto over the top of each fillet.
4. Press the breadcrumb mixture onto the pesto-covered side of the salmon fillets.
5. Place the salmon fillets in the air fryer basket, crust-side up.
6. Air fry for 10-12 minutes, or until the salmon is cooked through and the crust is golden brown.
7. Serve with lemon wedges for squeezing over the top.

Tip: Pair this salmon with a light side of roasted vegetables or a fresh green salad.

CHICKEN AND BROCCOLI ALFREDO

Prep: 15 Minutes | Cook: 25 Minutes | Makes: 4 Servings

Ingredients:
- 2 cups cooked pasta (such as penne or fettuccine)
- 2 cups cooked chicken, shredded
- 2 cups broccoli florets, steamed
- 1 cup Alfredo sauce (store-bought or homemade)
- 1/2 cup shredded mozzarella cheese
- 1/4 cup grated Parmesan cheese
- 1 tsp garlic powder
- Salt and pepper to taste
- Fresh parsley for garnish

Directions:

1. Preheat your Breville Smart Oven Air Fryer Pro to 375°F using the Bake function.

2. In a large mixing bowl, combine the cooked pasta, shredded chicken, steamed broccoli, Alfredo sauce, garlic powder, salt, and pepper.

3. Transfer the mixture to a baking dish and spread it out evenly.

4. Sprinkle the mozzarella and Parmesan cheeses over the top.

5. Bake for 20-25 minutes, or until the cheese is melted and bubbly.

6. Garnish with fresh parsley before serving.

Tip: Serve this dish with a side of garlic bread for a complete comfort meal.

CHICKEN FAJITAS

Prep: 15 Minutes | Cook: 15 Minutes | Makes: 4 Servings

Ingredients:

- 2 boneless, skinless chicken breasts, sliced into strips
- 1 red bell pepper, sliced
- 1 green bell pepper, sliced
- 1 onion, sliced
- 2 tbsp olive oil
- 2 tsp chili powder
- 1 tsp ground cumin
- 1 tsp smoked paprika
- 1/2 tsp garlic powder
- 1/2 tsp onion powder
- Salt and pepper to taste
- Flour tortillas for serving
- Toppings: sour cream, salsa, guacamole, shredded cheese

Directions:

1. Preheat your Breville Smart Oven Air Fryer Pro to 375°F using the Air Fry function.

2. In a large mixing bowl, toss the chicken strips, bell peppers, and onion with olive oil, chili powder, cumin, smoked paprika, garlic powder, onion powder, salt, and pepper.

3. Place the chicken and vegetables in the air fryer basket in a single layer.

4. Air fry for 12-15 minutes, shaking the basket halfway through, until the chicken is cooked through and the vegetables are tender.

5. Serve the fajita mixture with warm flour tortillas and your favorite toppings.

Tip: For a low-carb option, serve the fajitas in lettuce wraps instead of tortillas.

EGGPLANT ROLLATINI

Prep: 20 Minutes | Cook: 30 Minutes | Makes: 4 Servings

Ingredients:

- 2 large eggplants, sliced lengthwise into 1/4-inch thick slices
- 1 cup ricotta cheese
- 1 cup shredded mozzarella cheese, divided
- 1/4 cup grated Parmesan cheese
- 1 egg, beaten

- 1 tsp dried basil
- 1 tsp dried oregano
- Salt and pepper to taste
- 2 cups marinara sauce
- Fresh basil for garnish

Directions:

1. Preheat your Breville Smart Oven Air Fryer Pro to 375°F using the Bake function.

2. Lightly salt the eggplant slices and let them sit for 10 minutes to draw out excess moisture. Pat dry with paper towels.

3. In a mixing bowl, combine the ricotta cheese, 1/2 cup shredded mozzarella, Parmesan cheese, beaten egg, dried basil, dried oregano, salt, and pepper.

4. Spread a thin layer of marinara sauce in the bottom of a baking dish.

5. Place a spoonful of the ricotta mixture on one end of each eggplant slice and roll it up tightly.

6. Arrange the eggplant rolls seam-side down in the baking dish and top with the remaining marinara sauce.

7. Sprinkle the remaining mozzarella cheese over the top.

8. Bake for 25-30 minutes, or until the cheese is melted and the eggplant is tender.

9. Garnish with fresh basil before serving.

Tip: Serve this dish with a side of garlic bread or a green salad.

COCONUT–CRUSTED CHICKEN TENDERS

Prep: 15 Minutes | Cook: 15 Minutes | Makes: 4 Servings

Ingredients:

- 1 lb chicken tenders
- 1/2 cup all-purpose flour
- 2 large eggs, beaten
- 1 cup shredded coconut (sweetened or unsweetened)
- 1/2 cup panko breadcrumbs
- 1/2 tsp garlic powder
- 1/2 tsp smoked paprika
- Salt and pepper to taste
- Cooking spray
- Sweet chili sauce or honey mustard for serving

Directions:

1. Preheat your Breville Smart Oven Air Fryer Pro to 375°F using the Air Fry function.

2. Set up a breading station with three shallow dishes: one with flour, one with beaten eggs, and one with a mixture of shredded coconut, panko breadcrumbs, garlic powder, smoked paprika, salt, and pepper.

3. Dredge each chicken tender in flour, dip in the beaten eggs, and coat with the coconut-panko mixture.

4. Place the breaded chicken tenders in the air fryer basket and lightly spray with cooking spray.

5. Air fry for 12-15 minutes, turning halfway through, until the chicken is golden brown and cooked through.

6. Serve with sweet chili sauce or honey mustard for dipping.

Tip: For a tropical twist, serve the chicken tenders with a side of coconut rice and mango salsa.

Lemon Garlic Shrimp Skewers

Prep: 15 Minutes | Cook: 10 Minutes | Makes: 4 Servings

Ingredients:

- 1 lb large shrimp, peeled and deveined
- 2 tbsp olive oil
- 2 cloves garlic, minced
- Juice and zest of 1 lemon
- 1 tsp dried oregano
- Salt and pepper to taste
- Fresh parsley for garnish
- Lemon wedges for serving
- Wooden skewers, soaked in water for 30 minutes

Directions:

1. In a bowl, combine the olive oil, minced garlic, lemon juice, lemon zest, oregano, salt, and pepper.
2. Add the shrimp to the marinade and toss to coat. Let it marinate for 15 minutes.
3. Preheat your Breville Smart Oven Air Fryer Pro to 375°F using the Air Fry function.
4. Thread the shrimp onto the soaked skewers.
5. Place the skewers in the air fryer basket and air fry for 8-10 minutes, turning halfway through, until the shrimp are pink and cooked through.
6. Garnish with fresh parsley and serve with lemon wedges.

Tip: Serve these shrimp skewers with a side of couscous or a fresh salad for a complete meal.

Chicken Cordon Bleu

Prep: 20 Minutes | Cook: 25 Minutes | Makes: 4 Servings

Ingredients:

- 4 boneless, skinless chicken breasts
- 4 slices Swiss cheese
- 4 slices ham
- 1/2 cup breadcrumbs
- 1/4 cup grated Parmesan cheese
- 1 tbsp Dijon mustard
- 1 tbsp olive oil
- Salt and pepper to taste
- Toothpicks for securing

Directions:

1. Preheat your Breville Smart Oven Air Fryer Pro to 375°F using the Bake function.
2. Place a slice of Swiss cheese and a slice of ham on each chicken breast. Roll up the chicken and secure with toothpicks.
3. In a small bowl, mix together the breadcrumbs, Parmesan cheese, olive oil, salt, and pepper.
4. Brush each chicken roll with Dijon mustard, then coat with the breadcrumb mixture.
5. Place the chicken rolls in a greased baking dish and bake for 20-25 minutes, or until the chicken is cooked through and golden brown.
6. Remove the toothpicks before serving.

Tip: Serve this classic dish with a side of steamed vegetables or mashed potatoes.

TERIYAKI SALMON

Prep: 15 Minutes | Cook: 12 Minutes | Makes: 4 Servings

Ingredients:

- 4 salmon fillets
- 1/4 cup soy sauce
- 2 tbsp honey
- 1 tbsp rice vinegar
- 1 tbsp sesame oil
- 2 cloves garlic, minced
- 1 tsp grated ginger
- 1 tsp sesame seeds for garnish
- Chopped green onions for garnish

Directions:

1. In a small bowl, whisk together the soy sauce, honey, rice vinegar, sesame oil, garlic, and ginger.

2. Place the salmon fillets in a shallow dish and pour the marinade over them. Let them marinate for 15 minutes.

3. Preheat your Breville Smart Oven Air Fryer Pro to 375°F using the Air Fry function.

4. Place the salmon fillets in the air fryer basket, skin-side down, and air fry for 10-12 minutes, or until the salmon is cooked through and slightly caramelized on top.

5. Garnish with sesame seeds and chopped green onions before serving.

Tip: Serve the teriyaki salmon with steamed rice and stir-fried vegetables.

EGGPLANT PARMESAN

Prep: 20 Minutes | Cook: 30 Minutes | Makes: 4 Servings

Ingredients:

- 2 large eggplants, sliced into 1/4-inch rounds
- 1 cup breadcrumbs
- 1/2 cup grated Parmesan cheese
- 2 large eggs, beaten
- 2 cups marinara sauce
- 1 cup shredded mozzarella cheese
- 1/4 cup fresh basil, chopped
- Salt and pepper to taste
- Olive oil for drizzling

Directions:

1. Preheat your Breville Smart Oven Air Fryer Pro to 375°F using the Bake function.

2. In a shallow dish, combine the breadcrumbs, Parmesan cheese, salt, and pepper.

3. Dip each eggplant slice into the beaten eggs, then coat with the breadcrumb mixture.

4. Arrange the coated eggplant slices on a baking sheet and lightly drizzle with olive oil.

5. Bake for 20 minutes, flipping halfway through, until the eggplant is golden and crispy.

6. Spread a layer of marinara sauce in a baking dish, then layer the baked eggplant slices on top. Repeat with more sauce and eggplant slices, ending with a layer of sauce.

7. Sprinkle shredded mozzarella cheese on top and bake for an additional 10 minutes, or until the cheese is melted and bubbly.

Tip: Serve this eggplant Parmesan with a side of pasta or a green salad.

CHAPTER 4: SIDE DISHES

GARLIC PARMESAN ASPARAGUS

Prep: 10 Minutes | Cook: 10 Minutes | Makes: 4 Servings

Ingredients:

- 1 bunch asparagus, trimmed
- 2 tbsp olive oil
- 3 cloves garlic, minced
- 1/4 cup grated Parmesan cheese
- 1/2 tsp lemon zest
- Salt and pepper to taste
- Fresh parsley for garnish

Directions:

1. Preheat your Breville Smart Oven Air Fryer Pro to 375°F using the Air Fry function.
2. In a large bowl, toss the asparagus with olive oil, minced garlic, salt, and pepper.
3. Arrange the asparagus in the air fryer basket in a single layer.
4. Air fry for 8-10 minutes, shaking the basket halfway through, until the asparagus is tender and slightly crispy.
5. Sprinkle the cooked asparagus with grated Parmesan cheese and lemon zest.
6. Garnish with fresh parsley before serving.

Tip: Serve this dish with a squeeze of fresh lemon juice for added brightness.

SWEET POTATO WEDGES WITH CINNAMON

Prep: 10 Minutes | Cook: 25 Minutes | Makes: 4 Servings

Ingredients:

- 2 large sweet potatoes, cut into wedges
- 2 tbsp olive oil
- 1 tsp ground cinnamon
- 1 tbsp honey
- Salt to taste
- Fresh thyme leaves for garnish (optional)

Directions:

1. Preheat your Breville Smart Oven Air Fryer Pro to 400°F using the Bake function.
2. In a large bowl, toss the sweet potato wedges with olive oil, ground cinnamon, and salt.
3. Arrange the sweet potato wedges on a baking sheet in a single layer.
4. Bake for 20-25 minutes, flipping halfway through, until the wedges are golden and tender.
5. Drizzle the baked sweet potato wedges with honey.
6. Garnish with fresh thyme leaves if desired before serving.

Tip: For a spicy-sweet twist, sprinkle a pinch of cayenne pepper over the sweet potatoes before baking.

Brussels Sprouts with Balsamic Glaze

Prep: 10 Minutes | Cook: 12 Minutes | Makes: 4 Servings

Ingredients:

- 1 lb Brussels sprouts, trimmed and halved
- 2 tbsp olive oil
- Salt and pepper to taste
- 1/4 cup balsamic glaze
- 1/4 cup toasted pine nuts (optional)

Directions:

1. Preheat your Breville Smart Oven Air Fryer Pro to 375°F using the Air Fry function.
2. In a large bowl, toss the Brussels sprouts with olive oil, salt, and pepper.
3. Arrange the Brussels sprouts in the air fryer basket in a single layer.
4. Air fry for 10-12 minutes, shaking the basket halfway through, until the Brussels sprouts are crispy on the outside and tender on the inside.
5. Drizzle the Brussels sprouts with balsamic glaze.
6. Sprinkle with toasted pine nuts before serving, if desired.

Tip: For an extra burst of flavor, add a handful of dried cranberries to the dish before serving.

Cheddar and Chive Biscuits

Prep: 15 Minutes | Cook: 15 Minutes | Makes: 8 Biscuits

Ingredients:

- 2 cups all-purpose flour
- 1 tbsp baking powder
- 1/2 tsp salt
- 1/2 cup cold butter, cubed
- 1 cup shredded sharp cheddar cheese
- 2 tbsp chopped fresh chives
- 3/4 cup milk
- 1 egg, beaten (for egg wash)

Directions:

1. Preheat your Breville Smart Oven Air Fryer Pro to 400°F using the Bake function.
2. In a large bowl, whisk together the flour, baking powder, and salt.
3. Cut in the cold butter using a pastry cutter or your fingers until the mixture resembles coarse crumbs.
4. Stir in the shredded cheddar cheese and chopped chives.
5. Gradually add the milk, stirring just until the dough comes together.
6. Turn the dough out onto a floured surface and knead gently a few times. Pat the dough into a 1-inch thick round and cut out biscuits using a biscuit cutter.
7. Place the biscuits on a baking sheet and brush the tops with the beaten egg.
8. Bake for 12-15 minutes, or until the biscuits are golden brown.

Tip: These biscuits are perfect alongside soups, stews, or as part of a hearty breakfast.

Maple Glazed Carrots

Prep: 10 Minutes | Cook: 15 Minutes | Makes: 4 Servings

Ingredients:

- 1 lb baby carrots
- 2 tbsp olive oil
- 2 tbsp maple syrup
- 1 tsp Dijon mustard
- Salt and pepper to taste
- Fresh parsley for garnish

Directions:

1. Preheat your Breville Smart Oven Air Fryer Pro to 375°F using the Air Fry function.
2. In a large bowl, toss the baby carrots with olive oil, maple syrup, Dijon mustard, salt, and pepper.
3. Arrange the carrots in the air fryer basket in a single layer.
4. Air fry for 12-15 minutes, shaking the basket halfway through, until the carrots are tender and caramelized.
5. Garnish with fresh parsley before serving.

Tip: For a touch of spice, add a pinch of ground cinnamon or nutmeg to the glaze before air frying.

Zucchini Chips with Garlic Aioli

Prep: 10 Minutes | Cook: 15 Minutes | Makes: 4 Servings

Ingredients:

- 2 medium zucchinis, thinly sliced
- 1/2 cup panko breadcrumbs
- 1/4 cup grated Parmesan cheese
- 1 tsp garlic powder
- 1/2 tsp smoked paprika
- Salt and pepper to taste
- 1/4 cup all-purpose flour
- 2 large eggs, beaten
- Cooking spray

For the Garlic Aioli:

- 1/2 cup mayonnaise
- 1 clove garlic, minced
- 1 tbsp lemon juice
- Salt and pepper to taste

Directions:

1. Preheat your Breville Smart Oven Air Fryer Pro to 375°F using the Air Fry function.
2. In a shallow dish, mix the panko breadcrumbs, Parmesan cheese, garlic powder, smoked paprika, salt, and pepper.
3. Place the flour in another shallow dish and the beaten eggs in a third dish.
4. Dredge each zucchini slice in flour, dip in the beaten eggs, and coat with the breadcrumb mixture.
5. Arrange the zucchini slices in a single layer in the air fryer basket and lightly spray with cooking spray.

6. Air fry for 12-15 minutes, flipping halfway through, until the zucchini chips are golden and crispy.

7. In a small bowl, mix together the mayonnaise, minced garlic, lemon juice, salt, and pepper to make the garlic aioli.

8. Serve the zucchini chips warm with garlic aioli on the side.

Tip: For extra crunch, use a mandoline to slice the zucchini evenly.

Mediterranean Stuffed Tomatoes
Prep: 15 Minutes | Cook: 20 Minutes | Makes: 4 Servings

Ingredients:
- 4 large tomatoes
- 1/2 cup cooked quinoa
- 1/4 cup crumbled feta cheese
- 1/4 cup chopped Kalamata olives
- 2 tbsp chopped fresh basil
- 1 clove garlic, minced
- 2 tbsp olive oil
- Salt and pepper to taste
- Fresh basil leaves for garnish

Directions:
1. Preheat your Breville Smart Oven Air Fryer Pro to 375°F using the Bake function.
2. Slice the tops off the tomatoes and scoop out the seeds and pulp, leaving a hollow shell.
3. In a mixing bowl, combine the cooked quinoa, feta cheese, chopped olives, basil, minced garlic, olive oil, salt, and pepper.
4. Stuff each tomato with the quinoa mixture and place them in a baking dish.
5. Bake for 15-20 minutes, or until the tomatoes are tender and the filling is heated through.
6. Garnish with fresh basil leaves before serving.

Tip: Serve these stuffed tomatoes as a light side dish or as part of a Mediterranean-inspired meal.

Parmesan Crusted Cauliflower
Prep: 15 Minutes | Cook: 12 Minutes | Makes: 4 Servings

Ingredients:
- 1 small head of cauliflower, cut into florets
- 1/2 cup panko breadcrumbs
- 1/2 cup grated Parmesan cheese
- 1 tsp Italian seasoning
- 1/2 tsp garlic powder
- 2 large eggs, beaten
- Salt and pepper to taste
- Cooking spray

Directions:

1. Preheat your Breville Smart Oven Air Fryer Pro to 375°F using the Air Fry function.
2. In a shallow dish, mix the panko breadcrumbs, Parmesan cheese, Italian seasoning, garlic powder, salt, and pepper.
3. Dip each cauliflower floret in the beaten eggs, then coat with the breadcrumb mixture.
4. Arrange the cauliflower florets in a single layer in the air fryer basket and lightly spray with cooking spray.
5. Air fry for 10-12 minutes, shaking the basket halfway through, until the cauliflower is golden and crispy.
6. Serve immediately as a tasty and healthy side dish.

Tip: For added flavor, serve with a side of marinara sauce for dipping.

Cheesy Garlic Pull-Apart Bread

Prep: 10 Minutes | Cook: 15 Minutes | Makes: 4-6 Servings

Ingredients:

- 1 loaf of crusty bread (such as sourdough or Italian)
- 1/2 cup melted butter
- 3 cloves garlic, minced
- 1 cup shredded mozzarella cheese
- 1/4 cup grated Parmesan cheese
- 2 tbsp chopped fresh parsley
- 1 tsp Italian seasoning

Directions:

1. Preheat your Breville Smart Oven Air Fryer Pro to 375°F using the Bake function.
2. Slice the loaf of bread in a crisscross pattern, making sure not to cut all the way through.
3. In a small bowl, mix the melted butter, minced garlic, chopped parsley, and Italian seasoning.
4. Carefully pour the garlic butter mixture into the cuts of the bread, making sure to get it into all the crevices.
5. Stuff the shredded mozzarella and Parmesan cheese into the cuts of the bread.
6. Wrap the loaf in aluminum foil and bake for 10 minutes.
7. Unwrap the foil and bake for an additional 5 minutes, or until the cheese is melted and bubbly.
8. Serve warm and pull apart the bread pieces to enjoy.

Tip: This cheesy garlic bread pairs perfectly with pasta dishes or can be served as a crowd-pleasing appetizer.

Honey Glazed Carrots with Thyme

Prep: 10 Minutes | Cook: 12 Minutes | Makes: 4 Servings

Ingredients:
- 1 lb baby carrots
- 2 tbsp olive oil
- 2 tbsp honey
- 1 tsp fresh thyme leaves
- Salt and pepper to taste

Directions:
1. Preheat your Breville Smart Oven Air Fryer Pro to 375°F using the Air Fry function.
2. In a large bowl, toss the baby carrots with olive oil, honey, thyme, salt, and pepper.
3. Arrange the carrots in a single layer in the air fryer basket.
4. Air fry for 10-12 minutes, shaking the basket halfway through, until the carrots are tender and caramelized.
5. Serve immediately as a sweet and savory side dish.

Tip: For added depth of flavor, try using maple syrup instead of honey.

Crispy Green Beans with Lemon Zest

Prep: 10 Minutes | Cook: 10 Minutes | Makes: 4 Servings

Ingredients:
- 1 lb fresh green beans, trimmed
- 2 tbsp olive oil
- 1/2 cup panko breadcrumbs
- 1/4 cup grated Parmesan cheese
- 1 tsp garlic powder
- 1 tsp lemon zest
- Salt and pepper to taste
- Lemon wedges for serving

Directions:
1. Preheat your Breville Smart Oven Air Fryer Pro to 375°F using the Air Fry function.
2. In a large bowl, toss the green beans with olive oil, salt, and pepper.
3. In a separate bowl, mix the panko breadcrumbs, Parmesan cheese, garlic powder, and lemon zest.
4. Coat the green beans with the breadcrumb mixture, pressing lightly to adhere.
5. Arrange the green beans in a single layer in the air fryer basket.
6. Air fry for 8-10 minutes, shaking the basket halfway through, until the green beans are crispy and golden.
7. Serve with lemon wedges on the side for an extra burst of freshness.

Tip: These crispy green beans make a great alternative to fries or chips.

Corn Casserole with Cheddar and Jalapeños

Prep: 15 Minutes | Cook: 30 Minutes | Makes: 4-6 Servings

Ingredients:

- 1 can (15 oz) whole kernel corn, drained
- 1 can (15 oz) creamed corn
- 1 cup shredded cheddar cheese
- 1/2 cup sour cream
- 1/4 cup melted butter
- 1/2 cup diced jalapeños (seeded for less heat)
- 1/2 cup cornmeal
- 2 large eggs, beaten
- 1 tsp baking powder
- Salt and pepper to taste
- Fresh cilantro for garnish

Directions:

1. Preheat your Breville Smart Oven Air Fryer Pro to 375°F using the Bake function.

2. In a large mixing bowl, combine the whole kernel corn, creamed corn, shredded cheddar cheese, sour cream, melted butter, diced jalapeños, cornmeal, beaten eggs, baking powder, salt, and pepper.

3. Pour the mixture into a greased baking dish.

4. Bake for 25-30 minutes, or until the casserole is golden and set in the center.

5. Garnish with fresh cilantro before serving.

Tip: Serve this spicy and cheesy corn casserole alongside grilled meats or as a flavorful side for any meal.

Herb-Roasted Baby Potatoes

Prep: 10 Minutes | Cook: 20 Minutes | Makes: 4 Servings

Ingredients:

- 1 lb baby potatoes, halved
- 2 tbsp olive oil
- 1 tsp dried rosemary
- 1 tsp dried thyme
- 1/2 tsp garlic powder
- Salt and pepper to taste
- Fresh parsley for garnish

Directions:

1. Preheat your Breville Smart Oven Air Fryer Pro to 400°F using the Air Fry function.

2. In a large bowl, toss the halved baby potatoes with olive oil, rosemary, thyme, garlic powder, salt, and pepper.

3. Arrange the potatoes in a single layer in the air fryer basket.

4. Air fry for 18-20 minutes, shaking the basket halfway through, until the potatoes are crispy on the outside and tender on the inside.

5. Garnish with fresh parsley before serving.

Tip: For a zesty twist, add a sprinkle of lemon zest or a squeeze of lemon juice over the potatoes before serving.

Spinach and Artichoke Gratin

Prep: 15 Minutes | Cook: 20 Minutes | Makes: 4-6 Servings

Ingredients:

- 1 package (10 oz) frozen spinach, thawed and drained
- 1 can (14 oz) artichoke hearts, drained and chopped
- 1/2 cup cream cheese, softened
- 1/2 cup sour cream
- 1/4 cup grated Parmesan cheese
- 1/4 cup shredded mozzarella cheese
- 1 clove garlic, minced
- 1/2 cup panko breadcrumbs
- 2 tbsp melted butter
- Salt and pepper to taste

Directions:

1. Preheat your Breville Smart Oven Air Fryer Pro to 375°F using the Bake function.

2. In a large mixing bowl, combine the spinach, chopped artichoke hearts, cream cheese, sour cream, Parmesan cheese, mozzarella cheese, garlic, salt, and pepper.

3. Spread the mixture evenly in a baking dish.

4. In a separate bowl, mix the panko breadcrumbs with melted butter. Sprinkle the breadcrumb mixture over the spinach and artichoke mixture.

5. Bake for 18-20 minutes, or until the gratin is bubbly and the top is golden brown.

Tip: This gratin pairs well with roasted chicken or as part of a holiday spread.

Caramelized Onion and Goat Cheese Tartlets

Prep: 20 Minutes | Cook: 15 Minutes | Makes: 12 Tartlets

Ingredients:

- 1 sheet puff pastry, thawed
- 2 large onions, thinly sliced
- 2 tbsp butter
- 1 tbsp olive oil
- 1 tsp sugar
- 4 oz goat cheese, crumbled
- Fresh thyme leaves for garnish
- Salt and pepper to taste

Directions:

1. Preheat your Breville Smart Oven Air Fryer Pro to 375°F using the Air Fry function.

2. In a skillet, melt the butter and olive oil over medium heat. Add the sliced onions and sugar, and cook, stirring occasionally, until the onions are soft and caramelized, about 15 minutes. Season with salt and pepper.

3. Roll out the puff pastry on a floured surface and cut into 12 small squares.

4. Place the puff pastry squares in the air fryer basket, leaving space between each.

5. Top each square with a spoonful of caramelized onions and crumbled goat cheese.

6. Air fry for 10-12 minutes, or until the puff pastry is golden and the cheese is melted.

7. Garnish with fresh thyme leaves before serving.

Tip: These tartlets make an elegant side dish or appetizer for a dinner party.

Maple Bacon Brussels Sprouts

Prep: 10 Minutes | Cook: 15 Minutes | Makes: 4 Servings

Ingredients:

- 1 lb Brussels sprouts, trimmed and halved
- 4 slices bacon, chopped
- 2 tbsp maple syrup
- 1 tbsp olive oil
- Salt and pepper to taste

Directions:

1. Preheat your Breville Smart Oven Air Fryer Pro to 375°F using the Air Fry function.
2. In a large bowl, toss the Brussels sprouts with olive oil, salt, and pepper.
3. Place the chopped bacon and Brussels sprouts in the air fryer basket in a single layer.
4. Air fry for 12-15 minutes, shaking the basket halfway through, until the Brussels sprouts are crispy and the bacon is cooked.
5. Drizzle with maple syrup and toss to coat evenly.
6. Serve immediately for a sweet and savory side dish.

Tip: For extra flavor, add a splash of balsamic vinegar along with the maple syrup.

Cheesy Cauliflower Gratin

Prep: 15 Minutes | Cook: 25 Minutes | Makes: 4-6 Servings

Ingredients:

- 1 head cauliflower, cut into florets
- 1 cup shredded cheddar cheese
- 1/2 cup grated Parmesan cheese
- 1/2 cup heavy cream
- 2 tbsp butter
- 1 clove garlic, minced
- 1/2 tsp mustard powder
- Salt and pepper to taste
- 1/4 cup panko breadcrumbs

Directions:

1. Preheat your Breville Smart Oven Air Fryer Pro to 375°F using the Bake function.
2. Steam the cauliflower florets until just tender, about 5 minutes. Drain and set aside.
3. In a saucepan, melt the butter over medium heat. Add the minced garlic and sauté until fragrant.
4. Stir in the heavy cream, mustard powder, salt, and pepper. Heat until the mixture is just about to simmer.
5. Remove from heat and stir in the shredded cheddar and Parmesan cheese until melted and smooth.
6. Place the steamed cauliflower in a baking dish and pour the cheese sauce over the top. Stir to coat the cauliflower evenly.
7. Sprinkle the panko breadcrumbs over the top.
8. Bake for 20-25 minutes, or until the top is golden brown and the cheese is bubbly.
9. Serve warm.

Tip: Add a pinch of cayenne pepper to the cheese sauce for a subtle kick of heat.

CRISPY POLENTA FRIES

Prep: 10 Minutes | Cook: 15 Minutes | Makes: 4 Servings

Ingredients:

- 1 tube pre-cooked polenta
- 2 tbsp olive oil
- 1/4 cup grated Parmesan cheese
- 1 tsp garlic powder
- 1 tsp Italian seasoning
- Salt and pepper to taste
- Marinara sauce for dipping

Directions:

1. Preheat your Breville Smart Oven Air Fryer Pro to 400°F using the Air Fry function.
2. Slice the polenta into fry-shaped sticks, about 1/2-inch thick.
3. In a large bowl, toss the polenta sticks with olive oil, garlic powder, Italian seasoning, salt, and pepper.
4. Arrange the polenta fries in a single layer in the air fryer basket.
5. Air fry for 12-15 minutes, flipping halfway through, until the fries are crispy and golden.
6. Sprinkle with grated Parmesan cheese and serve with marinara sauce for dipping.

Tip: For a cheesy variation, add shredded mozzarella to the top of the fries during the last few minutes of cooking.

GARLIC BUTTER MUSHROOMS

Prep: 10 Minutes | Cook: 20 Minutes | Makes: 4 Servings

Ingredients:

- 1 lb cremini or white button mushrooms, cleaned and stems trimmed
- 1/4 cup butter, melted
- 3 cloves garlic, minced
- 1 tbsp soy sauce
- 1 tbsp fresh thyme leaves
- Salt and pepper to taste
- Fresh parsley for garnish

Directions:

1. Preheat your Breville Smart Oven Air Fryer Pro to 375°F using the Bake function.
2. In a mixing bowl, combine the melted butter, minced garlic, soy sauce, fresh thyme, salt, and pepper.
3. Toss the mushrooms in the garlic butter mixture until well coated.
4. Arrange the mushrooms in a baking dish in a single layer.
5. Bake for 15-20 minutes, or until the mushrooms are tender and golden brown.
6. Garnish with fresh parsley before serving.

Tip: These garlic butter mushrooms pair wonderfully with steak or grilled chicken.

Sweet Potato and Black Bean Salad

Prep: 15 Minutes | Cook: 20 Minutes | Makes: 4 Servings

Ingredients:

- 2 medium sweet potatoes, peeled and diced
- 1 can (15 oz) black beans, drained and rinsed
- 1/2 cup corn kernels (fresh or canned)
- 1/2 red onion, finely chopped
- 1 red bell pepper, diced
- 2 tbsp olive oil
- 1 tsp ground cumin
- 1/2 tsp smoked paprika
- Salt and pepper to taste
- 2 tbsp chopped fresh cilantro
- Lime wedges for serving

Directions:

1. Preheat your Breville Smart Oven Air Fryer Pro to 400°F using the Air Fry function.

2. In a large bowl, toss the diced sweet potatoes with olive oil, ground cumin, smoked paprika, salt, and pepper.

3. Arrange the sweet potatoes in a single layer in the air fryer basket.

4. Air fry for 15-20 minutes, shaking the basket halfway through, until the sweet potatoes are crispy on the outside and tender on the inside.

5. In a large mixing bowl, combine the air-fried sweet potatoes, black beans, corn, red onion, and red bell pepper.

6. Toss the salad with fresh cilantro and serve with lime wedges on the side.

Tip: For a complete meal, serve this salad over a bed of mixed greens or quinoa.

CHAPTER 5: DESSERTS

Cinnamon Sugar Churro Bites

Prep: 15 Minutes | Cook: 8 Minutes | Makes: 4 Servings

Ingredients:

- 1 can refrigerated biscuit dough
- 1/4 cup melted butter
- 1/2 cup granulated sugar
- 1 tbsp ground cinnamon
- Chocolate or caramel sauce for dipping (optional)

Directions:

1. Preheat your Breville Smart Oven Air Fryer Pro to 350°F using the Air Fry function.
2. Cut each biscuit into quarters and roll them into small balls.
3. Place the dough balls in the air fryer basket in a single layer, making sure they don't touch.
4. Air fry for 6-8 minutes, or until the churro bites are golden brown and puffed.
5. In a small bowl, mix together the sugar and cinnamon.
6. Brush the warm churro bites with melted butter, then roll them in the cinnamon sugar mixture until well coated.
7. Serve warm with chocolate or caramel sauce for dipping, if desired.

Tip: For an extra indulgence, drizzle the churro bites with melted chocolate before serving.

Apple Crisp with Oat Topping

Prep: 15 Minutes | Cook: 25 Minutes | Makes: 4 Servings

Ingredients:

- 4 large apples, peeled, cored, and sliced
- 1 tbsp lemon juice
- 1/4 cup granulated sugar
- 1/2 tsp ground cinnamon
- 1/4 tsp ground nutmeg
- 1/2 cup old-fashioned oats
- 1/2 cup all-purpose flour
- 1/4 cup brown sugar
- 1/4 cup cold butter, cubed
- Vanilla ice cream for serving (optional)

Directions:

1. Preheat your Breville Smart Oven Air Fryer Pro to 350°F using the Bake function.
2. In a large mixing bowl, toss the apple slices with lemon juice, granulated sugar, cinnamon, and nutmeg. Spread the apples evenly in a baking dish.
3. In a separate bowl, combine the oats, flour, brown sugar, and cold butter. Use your fingers or a pastry cutter to mix until the topping resembles coarse crumbs.
4. Sprinkle the oat mixture evenly over the apples.
5. Bake for 25-30 minutes, or until the topping is golden brown and the apples are tender.
6. Serve warm with vanilla ice cream, if desired.

Tip: Add a handful of chopped nuts to the topping for extra crunch.

Nutella-Stuffed Pastry Twists

Prep: 10 Minutes | Cook: 10 Minutes | Makes: 4 Servings

Ingredients:

- 1 sheet puff pastry, thawed
- 1/4 cup Nutella
- 1/4 cup chopped hazelnuts (optional)
- 1 egg, beaten (for egg wash)
- Powdered sugar for dusting

Directions:

1. Preheat your Breville Smart Oven Air Fryer Pro to 375°F using the Air Fry function.
2. Roll out the puff pastry sheet on a floured surface and cut it into 8 equal strips.
3. Spread a thin layer of Nutella down the center of each strip, leaving a small border around the edges.
4. Sprinkle chopped hazelnuts over the Nutella if desired.
5. Fold each strip in half lengthwise, enclosing the filling, and twist the pastry into a spiral shape.
6. Place the pastry twists in the air fryer basket, spacing them slightly apart.
7. Brush the tops with beaten egg and air fry for 8-10 minutes, or until the pastry is golden and puffed.
8. Dust with powdered sugar before serving.

Tip: Serve these warm with a cup of coffee or hot chocolate for a cozy treat.

Baked Berry Cobbler

Prep: 15 Minutes | Cook: 25 Minutes | Makes: 4 Servings

Ingredients:

- 2 cups mixed berries (such as blueberries, raspberries, and blackberries)
- 1/4 cup granulated sugar
- 1 tbsp cornstarch
- 1 tsp lemon juice
- 1/2 tsp vanilla extract
- 1 cup all-purpose flour
- 1/4 cup granulated sugar
- 1/4 cup brown sugar
- 1 tsp baking powder
- 1/4 tsp salt
- 1/2 cup cold butter, cubed
- 1/4 cup milk
- Vanilla ice cream or whipped cream for serving (optional)

Directions:

1. Preheat your Breville Smart Oven Air Fryer Pro to 375°F using the Bake function.
2. In a mixing bowl, toss the berries with sugar, cornstarch, lemon juice, and vanilla extract. Spread the berries evenly in a baking dish.
3. In a separate bowl, whisk together the flour, granulated sugar, brown sugar, baking powder, and salt.
4. Cut in the cold butter using a pastry cutter or your fingers until the mixture resembles coarse crumbs.
5. Stir in the milk until just combined, then drop spoonfuls of the dough over the berries.
6. Bake for 25-30 minutes, or until the topping is golden brown and the berries are bubbling.
7. Serve warm with vanilla ice cream or whipped cream, if desired.

Tip: Add a pinch of cinnamon to the dough for a hint of spice.

Chocolate Lava Cakes

Prep: 10 Minutes | Cook: 12 Minutes | Makes: 4 Servings

Ingredients:

- 1/2 cup unsalted butter
- 4 oz semi-sweet chocolate, chopped
- 1/2 cup powdered sugar
- 2 large eggs
- 2 egg yolks
- 1/4 cup all-purpose flour
- 1/2 tsp vanilla extract
- Pinch of salt
- Cocoa powder for dusting
- Vanilla ice cream for serving (optional)

Directions:

1. Preheat your Breville Smart Oven Air Fryer Pro to 375°F using the Air Fry function.
2. In a microwave-safe bowl, melt the butter and chopped chocolate together, stirring until smooth.
3. Whisk in the powdered sugar until well combined, then whisk in the eggs and egg yolks.
4. Stir in the flour, vanilla extract, and salt until just combined.
5. Grease four ramekins and dust the insides with cocoa powder.
6. Divide the batter evenly among the ramekins and place them in the air fryer basket.
7. Air fry for 10-12 minutes, or until the edges are set but the centers are still soft.
8. Let the cakes cool for 1 minute, then carefully invert onto serving plates.
9. Serve warm with a scoop of vanilla ice cream.

Tip: For a flavor twist, add a tablespoon of espresso powder to the batter for a mocha-flavored lava cake.

Banana Fritters with Honey Drizzle

Prep: 10 Minutes | Cook: 8 Minutes | Makes: 4 Servings

Ingredients:

- 2 ripe bananas, mashed
- 1/2 cup all-purpose flour
- 1/4 cup milk
- 1 egg, beaten
- 2 tbsp sugar
- 1 tsp baking powder
- 1/2 tsp ground cinnamon
- Pinch of salt
- Honey for drizzling
- Powdered sugar for dusting

Directions:

1. Preheat your Breville Smart Oven Air Fryer Pro to 350°F using the Air Fry function.
2. In a mixing bowl, combine the mashed bananas, flour, milk, egg, sugar, baking powder, cinnamon, and salt until a thick batter forms.

3. Drop spoonfuls of the batter into the air fryer basket, leaving space between each fritter.
4. Air fry for 6-8 minutes, flipping halfway through, until the fritters are golden and cooked through.
5. Drizzle the warm fritters with honey and dust with powdered sugar before serving.

Tip: For an extra treat, serve these fritters with a scoop of vanilla ice cream.

PEARS WITH CINNAMON AND WALNUTS
Prep: 10 Minutes | Cook: 20 Minutes | Makes: 4 Servings

Ingredients:

- 4 ripe pears, halved and cored
- 1/4 cup chopped walnuts
- 2 tbsp honey
- 1 tsp ground cinnamon
- 2 tbsp butter, melted
- Vanilla yogurt or ice cream for serving (optional)

Directions:

1. Preheat your Breville Smart Oven Air Fryer Pro to 375°F using the Bake function.
2. Place the pear halves in a baking dish, cut-side up.
3. In a small bowl, mix together the chopped walnuts, honey, cinnamon, and melted butter.
4. Spoon the walnut mixture into the center of each pear half.
5. Bake for 20-25 minutes, or until the pears are tender and the topping is golden.
6. Serve warm with a dollop of vanilla yogurt or ice cream, if desired.

Tip: For a crunchy contrast, add a sprinkle of granola on top before serving.

COCONUT MACAROONS
Prep: 10 Minutes | Cook: 12 Minutes | Makes: 12 Macaroons

Ingredients:

- 2 1/2 cups sweetened shredded coconut
- 1/2 cup sweetened condensed milk
- 1 tsp vanilla extract
- 2 large egg whites
- 1/4 tsp salt
- 1/2 cup melted dark chocolate (optional)

Directions:

1. Preheat your Breville Smart Oven Air Fryer Pro to 325°F using the Air Fry function.
2. In a large mixing bowl, combine the shredded coconut, sweetened condensed milk, and vanilla extract.
3. In a separate bowl, beat the egg whites with salt until stiff peaks form.
4. Gently fold the egg whites into the coconut mixture until fully combined.
5. Drop spoonfuls of the mixture onto a parchment-lined air fryer basket, shaping them into mounds.
6. Air fry for 10-12 minutes, or until the macaroons are golden brown on the outside.
7. Let the macaroons cool completely, then dip the bottoms in melted dark chocolate if desired.

8. Place the macaroons on a parchment-lined baking sheet until the chocolate sets.

Tip: Store these macaroons in an airtight container for up to a week.

Lemon Ricotta Cheesecake Bars
Prep: 15 Minutes | Cook: 30 Minutes | Makes: 9 Bars

Ingredients:
- 1 cup ricotta cheese
- 1/2 cup cream cheese, softened
- 1/4 cup granulated sugar
- 2 large eggs
- 1/4 cup lemon juice
- 1 tbsp lemon zest
- 1/2 tsp vanilla extract
- 1 cup crushed graham crackers
- 3 tbsp melted butter

Directions:
1. Preheat your Breville Smart Oven Air Fryer Pro to 350°F using the Bake function.
2. In a small bowl, mix the crushed graham crackers with melted butter. Press the mixture into the bottom of a greased 8x8-inch baking dish to form the crust.
3. In a large mixing bowl, beat the ricotta cheese, cream cheese, and sugar until smooth.
4. Add the eggs, one at a time, beating well after each addition.
5. Stir in the lemon juice, lemon zest, and vanilla extract.
6. Pour the ricotta mixture over the graham cracker crust and smooth the top.
7. Bake for 25-30 minutes, or until the center is set and the edges are lightly golden.
8. Let the bars cool completely before cutting into squares.

Tip: Dust the top with powdered sugar or garnish with fresh berries before serving.

Peach Hand Pies
Prep: 15 Minutes | Cook: 10 Minutes | Makes: 8 Hand Pies

Ingredients:
- 1 sheet puff pastry, thawed
- 2 ripe peaches, peeled, pitted, and diced
- 1/4 cup granulated sugar
- 1 tbsp cornstarch
- 1/2 tsp ground cinnamon
- 1/2 tsp vanilla extract
- 1 egg, beaten (for egg wash)
- Powdered sugar for dusting

Directions:
1. Preheat your Breville Smart Oven Air Fryer Pro to 375°F using the Air Fry function.
2. In a bowl, toss the diced peaches with sugar, cornstarch, cinnamon, and vanilla extract until well coated.

3. Roll out the puff pastry on a floured surface and cut it into 8 equal squares.

4. Spoon a small amount of the peach filling onto one side of each pastry square, leaving a border around the edges.

5. Fold the pastry over the filling to form a triangle and press the edges with a fork to seal.

6. Place the hand pies in the air fryer basket and brush the tops with the beaten egg.

7. Air fry for 8-10 minutes, or until the pies are golden and puffed.

8. Dust with powdered sugar before serving.

Tip: Serve these hand pies warm with a scoop of vanilla ice cream for a delicious summer treat.

STRAWBERRY CHEESECAKE CHIMICHANGAS

Prep: 15 Minutes | Cook: 8 Minutes | Makes: 4 Servings

Ingredients:

- 4 large flour tortillas
- 8 oz cream cheese, softened
- 1/4 cup powdered sugar
- 1 tsp vanilla extract
- 1 cup fresh strawberries, chopped
- 1/4 cup granulated sugar
- 1/2 tsp ground cinnamon
- Cooking spray
- Whipped cream for serving (optional)

Directions:

1. Preheat your Breville Smart Oven Air Fryer Pro to 375°F using the Air Fry function.

2. In a mixing bowl, beat the cream cheese, powdered sugar, and vanilla extract until smooth.

3. Spread a generous amount of the cream cheese mixture down the center of each tortilla.

4. Top with chopped strawberries, then roll up the tortillas tightly, tucking in the sides to form chimichangas.

5. In a small bowl, mix the granulated sugar and cinnamon.

6. Lightly spray the chimichangas with cooking spray and roll them in the cinnamon-sugar mixture.

7. Place the chimichangas in the air fryer basket, seam-side down, and air fry for 6-8 minutes, or until golden and crispy.

8. Serve warm with whipped cream, if desired.

Tip: For an extra indulgence, drizzle the chimichangas with chocolate sauce before serving.

Baked Caramel Apple Crumble

Prep: 15 Minutes | Cook: 25 Minutes | Makes: 4 Servings

Ingredients:

- 4 large apples, peeled, cored, and sliced
- 1/2 cup caramel sauce
- 1/2 cup all-purpose flour
- 1/2 cup old-fashioned oats
- 1/4 cup brown sugar
- 1/2 tsp ground cinnamon
- 1/4 cup cold butter, cubed
- Vanilla ice cream for serving (optional)

Directions:

1. Preheat your Breville Smart Oven Air Fryer Pro to 350°F using the Bake function.
2. In a baking dish, toss the sliced apples with the caramel sauce until evenly coated.
3. In a separate bowl, mix the flour, oats, brown sugar, and cinnamon.
4. Cut in the cold butter using a pastry cutter or your fingers until the mixture resembles coarse crumbs.
5. Sprinkle the crumble mixture evenly over the apples.
6. Bake for 25-30 minutes, or until the topping is golden and the apples are tender.
7. Serve warm with vanilla ice cream, if desired.

Tip: Add a handful of chopped pecans or walnuts to the crumble topping for extra crunch.

Lemon Blueberry Scones

Prep: 15 Minutes | Cook: 12 Minutes | Makes: 8 Scones

Ingredients:

- 2 cups all-purpose flour
- 1/4 cup granulated sugar
- 1 tbsp baking powder
- 1/2 tsp salt
- 1/2 cup cold butter, cubed
- 1/2 cup buttermilk
- 1 large egg
- 1 tsp lemon zest
- 1 cup fresh blueberries
- 1 egg, beaten (for egg wash)
- Lemon glaze (optional): 1 cup powdered sugar, 2 tbsp lemon juice

Directions:

1. Preheat your Breville Smart Oven Air Fryer Pro to 350°F using the Air Fry function.
2. In a large mixing bowl, whisk together the flour, sugar, baking powder, and salt.
3. Cut in the cold butter until the mixture resembles coarse crumbs.
4. In a separate bowl, whisk together the buttermilk, egg, and lemon zest.
5. Add the wet ingredients to the dry ingredients and mix until just combined.
6. Gently fold in the blueberries.
7. Turn the dough out onto a floured surface and shape it into a circle about 1-inch thick. Cut into 8 wedges.
8. Place the scones in the air fryer basket and brush the tops with the beaten egg.

9. Air fry for 10-12 minutes, or until the scones are golden and cooked through.

10. If desired, drizzle the scones with lemon glaze before serving.

Tip: Serve these scones with clotted cream or a dollop of lemon curd for a delightful treat.

CHOCOLATE BREAD PUDDING

Prep: 15 Minutes | Cook: 30 Minutes | Makes: 4-6 Servings

Ingredients:

- 4 cups cubed day-old bread (such as brioche or challah)
- 1/2 cup semi-sweet chocolate chips
- 2 cups milk
- 1/4 cup cocoa powder
- 1/2 cup granulated sugar
- 2 large eggs
- 1 tsp vanilla extract
- Whipped cream for serving (optional)

Directions:

1. Preheat your Breville Smart Oven Air Fryer Pro to 350°F using the Bake function.

2. Grease a baking dish and arrange the cubed bread in an even layer.

3. Sprinkle the chocolate chips over the bread.

4. In a saucepan, heat the milk, cocoa powder, and sugar over medium heat until warm (do not boil).

5. In a separate bowl, whisk the eggs and vanilla extract.

6. Slowly whisk the warm milk mixture into the eggs until combined.

7. Pour the custard mixture over the bread and chocolate chips, pressing down gently to ensure the bread is soaked.

8. Bake for 25-30 minutes, or until the pudding is set and the top is slightly crispy.

9. Serve warm with whipped cream, if desired.

Tip: Add a drizzle of caramel sauce over the top for an extra decadent touch.

Pineapple Coconut Upside-Down Cake

Prep: 15 Minutes | Cook: 20 Minutes | Makes: 6 Servings

Ingredients:

- 1/4 cup unsalted butter, melted
- 1/2 cup brown sugar
- 6 pineapple rings (fresh or canned)
- 6 maraschino cherries
- 1/2 cup sweetened shredded coconut
- 1/2 cup granulated sugar
- 1 large egg
- 1/4 cup pineapple juice
- 1/2 cup all-purpose flour
- 1/2 tsp baking powder
- Pinch of salt

Directions:

1. Preheat your Breville Smart Oven Air Fryer Pro to 350°F using the Air Fry function.

2. In a small bowl, mix the melted butter and brown sugar. Pour the mixture into the bottom of a greased 7-inch round cake pan.

3. Arrange the pineapple rings over the brown sugar mixture and place a maraschino cherry in the center of each ring.

4. Sprinkle the shredded coconut over the pineapple rings.

5. In a mixing bowl, beat the granulated sugar and egg until light and fluffy.

6. Stir in the pineapple juice.

7. In a separate bowl, whisk together the flour, baking powder, and salt. Gradually add the dry ingredients to the wet ingredients, mixing until just combined.

8. Pour the batter over the pineapple and coconut layer in the cake pan.

9. Air fry for 18-20 minutes, or until the cake is golden and a toothpick inserted into the center comes out clean.

10. Let the cake cool for 5 minutes, then carefully invert onto a serving plate.

Tip: Serve this tropical dessert with a dollop of whipped cream or a scoop of coconut ice cream.

Chapter 6: Healthy Dishes

Salmon with Avocado Salsa

Prep: 15 Minutes | Cook: 12 Minutes | Makes: 4 Servings

Ingredients:

- 4 salmon fillets
- 1 tbsp olive oil
- 1 tsp smoked paprika
- 1 tsp garlic powder
- Salt and pepper to taste
- 2 ripe avocados, diced
- 1/2 red onion, finely chopped
- 1 jalapeño, seeded and diced
- 1/4 cup fresh cilantro, chopped
- Juice of 1 lime

Directions:

1. Preheat your Breville Smart Oven Air Fryer Pro to 400°F using the Air Fry function.
2. Rub the salmon fillets with olive oil, smoked paprika, garlic powder, salt, and pepper.
3. Place the salmon fillets in the air fryer basket, skin-side down.
4. Air fry for 10-12 minutes, or until the salmon is cooked through and flakes easily with a fork.
5. While the salmon is cooking, prepare the avocado salsa by mixing the diced avocados, red onion, jalapeño, cilantro, and lime juice in a bowl.
6. Serve the salmon topped with the fresh avocado salsa.

Tip: This dish pairs well with a side of quinoa or a fresh green salad.

Quinoa-Stuffed Bell Peppers

Prep: 15 Minutes | Cook: 25 Minutes | Makes: 4 Servings

Ingredients:

- 4 large bell peppers, tops cut off and seeds removed
- 1 cup cooked quinoa
- 1 can (15 oz) black beans, drained and rinsed
- 1 cup diced tomatoes
- 1/2 cup corn kernels (fresh or frozen)
- 1 tsp ground cumin
- 1/2 tsp smoked paprika
- Salt and pepper to taste
- 1/4 cup shredded low-fat cheese (optional)
- Fresh cilantro for garnish

Directions:

1. Preheat your Breville Smart Oven Air Fryer Pro to 375°F using the Bake function.
2. In a large bowl, mix together the cooked quinoa, black beans, diced tomatoes, corn, ground cumin, smoked paprika, salt, and pepper.
3. Stuff the bell peppers with the quinoa mixture and place them in a baking dish.
4. Sprinkle with shredded cheese if using.
5. Bake for 20-25 minutes, or until the peppers are tender and the filling is heated through.
6. Garnish with fresh cilantro before serving.

Tip: For added flavor, serve with a dollop of Greek yogurt or guacamole.

Falafel with Tahini Sauce
Prep: 15 Minutes (plus soaking time) | Cook: 12 Minutes | Makes: 4 Servings

Ingredients:

- 1 cup dried chickpeas, soaked overnight and drained
- 1/2 onion, roughly chopped
- 2 cloves garlic, minced
- 1/4 cup fresh parsley, chopped
- 1 tsp ground cumin
- 1 tsp ground coriander
- 1/2 tsp baking powder
- Salt and pepper to taste
- 2 tbsp olive oil
- 1/4 cup tahini
- 2 tbsp lemon juice
- 1 clove garlic, minced
- Water as needed

Directions:

1. Preheat your Breville Smart Oven Air Fryer Pro to 375°F using the Air Fry function.
2. In a food processor, combine the soaked chickpeas, onion, garlic, parsley, cumin, coriander, baking powder, salt, and pepper. Pulse until the mixture is finely ground but not pureed.
3. Form the mixture into small balls or patties.
4. Brush the falafel with olive oil and place them in the air fryer basket.
5. Air fry for 10-12 minutes, turning halfway through, until the falafel are golden and crispy.
6. In a small bowl, whisk together the tahini, lemon juice, minced garlic, and enough water to reach your desired consistency.
7. Serve the falafel with the tahini sauce and a side of fresh salad or pita bread.

Tip: For a spicier falafel, add a pinch of cayenne pepper to the mixture before air frying.

Lemon Herb Chicken with Roasted Vegetables
Prep: 15 Minutes | Cook: 30 Minutes | Makes: 4 Servings

Ingredients:

- 4 boneless, skinless chicken breasts
- 2 tbsp olive oil
- Juice and zest of 1 lemon
- 2 cloves garlic, minced
- 1 tsp dried oregano
- 1 tsp dried thyme
- Salt and pepper to taste
- 1 lb baby potatoes, halved
- 1 cup baby carrots
- 1 red bell pepper, sliced

Directions:

1. Preheat your Breville Smart Oven Air Fryer Pro to 375°F using the Bake function.
2. In a small bowl, mix together the olive oil, lemon juice, lemon zest, minced garlic, oregano, thyme, salt, and pepper.
3. Place the chicken breasts in a baking dish and brush them with the lemon herb mixture.
4. Toss the baby potatoes, carrots, and bell pepper with the remaining lemon herb mixture and arrange them around the chicken in the baking dish.
5. Bake for 25-30 minutes, or until the chicken is cooked through and the vegetables are tender.
6. Serve the chicken and vegetables with an extra squeeze of lemon juice.

Tip: Add a handful of cherry tomatoes to the vegetable mix for a burst of color and flavor.

Zucchini Noodles with Pesto

Prep: 10 Minutes | Cook: 8 Minutes | Makes: 4 Servings

Ingredients:

- 4 medium zucchinis, spiralized into noodles
- 2 tbsp olive oil
- 1 cup cherry tomatoes, halved
- 1/4 cup pesto sauce (store-bought or homemade)
- Salt and pepper to taste
- Grated Parmesan cheese for serving (optional)

Directions:

1. Preheat your Breville Smart Oven Air Fryer Pro to 375°F using the Air Fry function.
2. In a large bowl, toss the zucchini noodles with olive oil, salt, and pepper.
3. Place the zucchini noodles in the air fryer basket and air fry for 6-8 minutes, shaking the basket halfway through, until the noodles are tender but still firm (al dente).
4. In the last 2 minutes of cooking, add the halved cherry tomatoes to the air fryer basket.
5. Toss the cooked zucchini noodles and tomatoes with the pesto sauce.
6. Serve immediately, topped with grated Parmesan cheese if desired.

Tip: For added protein, top the dish with grilled chicken or shrimp.

Tofu and Vegetable Stir-Fry

Prep: 15 Minutes | Cook: 15 Minutes | Makes: 4 Servings

Ingredients:

- 1 block (14 oz) firm tofu, drained and cubed
- 2 tbsp soy sauce
- 1 tbsp sesame oil
- 1 tbsp rice vinegar
- 1 tsp grated ginger
- 2 cloves garlic, minced
- 1 red bell pepper, sliced
- 1 yellow bell pepper, sliced
- 1 zucchini, sliced

- 1 cup broccoli florets
- 1/4 cup low-sodium soy sauce
- 1 tbsp hoisin sauce
- 1 tbsp honey
- 1 tsp cornstarch mixed with 1 tbsp water
- Cooked brown rice for serving
- Sesame seeds and chopped green onions for garnish

Directions:

1. Preheat your Breville Smart Oven Air Fryer Pro to 375°F using the Air Fry function.
2. In a small bowl, mix together the soy sauce, sesame oil, rice vinegar, grated ginger, and minced garlic.
3. Toss the tofu cubes in the marinade and let them sit for 10 minutes.
4. Place the marinated tofu in the air fryer basket and air fry for 12-15 minutes, shaking the basket halfway through, until the tofu is golden and crispy.
5. While the tofu is cooking, stir-fry the bell peppers, zucchini, and broccoli in a large skillet until tender-crisp.
6. In a small bowl, mix together the soy sauce, hoisin sauce, honey, and cornstarch slurry.
7. Add the cooked tofu to the skillet with the vegetables and pour the sauce over everything.
8. Cook for an additional 2-3 minutes, stirring to coat the tofu and vegetables evenly.
9. Serve the stir-fry over cooked brown rice, garnished with sesame seeds and chopped green onions.

Tip: Add a dash of chili flakes or Sriracha for some heat.

Baked Mediterranean Cod with Lemon
Prep: 10 Minutes | Cook: 20 Minutes | Makes: 4 Servings

Ingredients:
- 4 cod fillets
- 2 tbsp olive oil
- Juice and zest of 1 lemon
- 2 cloves garlic, minced
- 1 tsp dried oregano
- Salt and pepper to taste
- 1/2 cup pitted Kalamata olives, halved
- 1/2 cup cherry tomatoes, halved
- Fresh parsley for garnish

Directions:

1. Preheat your Breville Smart Oven Air Fryer Pro to 375°F using the Bake function.
2. In a small bowl, whisk together the olive oil, lemon juice, lemon zest, minced garlic, oregano, salt, and pepper.
3. Place the cod fillets in a baking dish and brush them with the lemon herb mixture.
4. Scatter the Kalamata olives and cherry tomatoes around the cod.
5. Bake for 15-20 minutes, or until the cod is cooked through and flakes easily with a fork.
6. Garnish with fresh parsley before serving.

Tip: Serve with a side of steamed vegetables or a simple salad for a light, healthy meal.

Spicy Chickpea and Avocado Salad

Prep: 10 Minutes | Cook: 12 Minutes | Makes: 4 Servings

Ingredients:

- 1 can (15 oz) chickpeas, drained and rinsed
- 1 tbsp olive oil
- 1 tsp smoked paprika
- 1/2 tsp ground cumin
- 1/4 tsp cayenne pepper
- Salt and pepper to taste
- 2 avocados, diced
- 1/2 red onion, thinly sliced
- 2 cups mixed greens
- 1/4 cup fresh cilantro, chopped
- Juice of 1 lime

Directions:

1. Preheat your Breville Smart Oven Air Fryer Pro to 375°F using the Air Fry function.
2. In a bowl, toss the chickpeas with olive oil, smoked paprika, cumin, cayenne pepper, salt, and pepper.
3. Place the chickpeas in the air fryer basket and air fry for 10-12 minutes, shaking the basket halfway through, until the chickpeas are crispy.
4. In a large bowl, combine the mixed greens, diced avocado, red onion, and cilantro.
5. Add the crispy chickpeas to the salad.
6. Drizzle with lime juice and toss to combine.
7. Serve immediately.

Tip: For added protein, top the salad with grilled chicken or shrimp.

Garlic and Herb Cauliflower Steaks

Prep: 10 Minutes | Cook: 15 Minutes | Makes: 4 Servings

Ingredients:

- 1 large head of cauliflower
- 2 tbsp olive oil
- 2 cloves garlic, minced
- 1 tsp dried thyme
- 1 tsp dried rosemary
- 1/2 tsp smoked paprika
- Salt and pepper to taste
- Fresh parsley for garnish

Directions:

1. Preheat your Breville Smart Oven Air Fryer Pro to 375°F using the Air Fry function.
2. Remove the outer leaves and stem from the cauliflower, keeping the core intact. Slice the cauliflower into 1-inch thick "steaks."
3. In a small bowl, mix together the olive oil, minced garlic, thyme, rosemary, smoked paprika, salt, and pepper.

4. Brush both sides of the cauliflower steaks with the garlic herb mixture.
5. Place the cauliflower steaks in the air fryer basket in a single layer.
6. Air fry for 12-15 minutes, flipping halfway through, until the cauliflower is tender and golden brown.
7. Garnish with fresh parsley before serving.

Tip: Serve these cauliflower steaks with a side of quinoa or a light salad for a complete meal.

CAULIFLOWER BUFFALO BITES
Prep: 10 Minutes | Cook: 15 Minutes | Makes: 4 Servings

Ingredients:

- 1 medium head of cauliflower, cut into florets
- 1/2 cup all-purpose flour (or chickpea flour)
- 1/2 cup water
- 1 tsp garlic powder
- 1 tsp smoked paprika
- Salt and pepper to taste
- 1/2 cup hot sauce (like Frank's RedHot)
- 1 tbsp melted butter (optional)
- 1 tbsp honey (optional)
- Fresh celery sticks and ranch dressing for serving

Directions:
1. Preheat your Breville Smart Oven Air Fryer Pro to 375°F using the Air Fry function.
2. In a large bowl, whisk together the flour, water, garlic powder, smoked paprika, salt, and pepper until a smooth batter forms.
3. Toss the cauliflower florets in the batter until well coated.
4. Place the battered cauliflower in the air fryer basket in a single layer.
5. Air fry for 12-15 minutes, shaking the basket halfway through, until the cauliflower is crispy and golden.
6. In a separate bowl, mix together the hot sauce, melted butter, and honey (if using).
7. Toss the crispy cauliflower bites in the hot sauce mixture until well coated.
8. Serve immediately with celery sticks and ranch dressing.

Tip: For a vegan option, skip the butter and honey, or replace the honey with maple syrup.

BAKED LEMON HERB QUINOA SALAD
Prep: 10 Minutes | Cook: 20 Minutes | Makes: 4 Servings

Ingredients:

- 1 cup quinoa, rinsed
- 2 cups vegetable broth or water
- 1 cucumber, diced
- 1/2 cup cherry tomatoes, halved
- 1/4 cup red onion, finely chopped
- 1/4 cup Kalamata olives, halved
- 1/4 cup crumbled feta cheese
- 2 tbsp fresh parsley, chopped
- 2 tbsp olive oil
- Juice and zest of 1 lemon

- Salt and pepper to taste

Directions:

1. Preheat your Breville Smart Oven Air Fryer Pro to 375°F using the Bake function.

2. In a medium saucepan, bring the vegetable broth or water to a boil. Add the quinoa, reduce the heat, cover, and simmer for 15 minutes, or until the quinoa is cooked and the liquid is absorbed. Fluff with a fork and let cool.

3. In a large mixing bowl, combine the cooked quinoa, cucumber, cherry tomatoes, red onion, olives, feta cheese, and parsley.

4. In a small bowl, whisk together the olive oil, lemon juice, lemon zest, salt, and pepper.

5. Pour the dressing over the quinoa salad and toss to combine.

6. Serve chilled or at room temperature.

Tip: For added protein, top the salad with grilled chicken or chickpeas.

ZUCCHINI PARMESAN CHIPS

Prep: 10 Minutes | Cook: 12 Minutes | Makes: 4 Servings

Ingredients:

- 2 medium zucchinis, thinly sliced
- 1/2 cup panko breadcrumbs
- 1/4 cup grated Parmesan cheese
- 1 tsp Italian seasoning
- 1/2 tsp garlic powder
- Salt and pepper to taste
- 1/4 cup all-purpose flour
- 2 large eggs, beaten
- Cooking spray
- Marinara sauce for dipping

Directions:

1. Preheat your Breville Smart Oven Air Fryer Pro to 375°F using the Air Fry function.

2. In a shallow dish, mix the panko breadcrumbs, Parmesan cheese, Italian seasoning, garlic powder, salt, and pepper.

3. Place the flour in a separate shallow dish and the beaten eggs in another.

4. Dredge each zucchini slice in flour, dip in the beaten eggs, and then coat with the breadcrumb mixture.

5. Place the breaded zucchini slices in a single layer in the air fryer basket and lightly spray with cooking spray.

6. Air fry for 10-12 minutes, flipping halfway through, until the zucchini chips are crispy and golden.

7. Serve immediately with marinara sauce for dipping.

Tip: For a gluten-free option, use gluten-free breadcrumbs and flour.

Sweet Potato and Kale Frittata

Prep: 15 Minutes | Cook: 20 Minutes | Makes: 4 Servings

Ingredients:

- 1 medium sweet potato, peeled and diced
- 1 tbsp olive oil
- 1 small onion, finely chopped
- 2 cups chopped kale, stems removed
- 8 large eggs
- 1/4 cup milk (or plant-based milk)
- 1/4 cup crumbled goat cheese (optional)
- Salt and pepper to taste
- Fresh herbs for garnish (optional)

Directions:

1. Preheat your Breville Smart Oven Air Fryer Pro to 375°F using the Bake function.
2. Toss the diced sweet potato with olive oil, salt, and pepper. Spread on a baking sheet and bake for 15 minutes, or until tender.
3. In a large skillet, sauté the onion until soft. Add the chopped kale and cook until wilted.
4. In a mixing bowl, whisk together the eggs, milk, salt, and pepper.
5. Stir in the roasted sweet potato, sautéed onion, and kale. Add the crumbled goat cheese if using.
6. Pour the mixture into a greased baking dish.
7. Bake for 20-25 minutes, or until the frittata is set and golden brown on top.
8. Garnish with fresh herbs before serving.

Tip: This frittata is perfect for meal prep and can be enjoyed hot or cold.

Sesame-Crusted Tofu with Steamed Broccoli

Prep: 15 Minutes | Cook: 15 Minutes | Makes: 4 Servings

Ingredients:

- 1 block (14 oz) firm tofu, drained and pressed
- 2 tbsp soy sauce
- 1 tbsp sesame oil
- 1 tbsp rice vinegar
- 1 tbsp maple syrup
- 2 tbsp sesame seeds
- 1 bunch broccoli, cut into florets
- 1 tbsp olive oil
- Salt and pepper to taste
- Cooked brown rice for serving
- Sliced green onions and sesame seeds for garnish

Directions:

1. Preheat your Breville Smart Oven Air Fryer Pro to 375°F using the Air Fry function.
2. Cut the tofu into slices or cubes.

3. In a small bowl, mix together the soy sauce, sesame oil, rice vinegar, and maple syrup. Toss the tofu in the marinade and let it sit for 10 minutes.

4. Press the sesame seeds onto the tofu pieces, coating them evenly.

5. Place the tofu in the air fryer basket and air fry for 12-15 minutes, turning halfway through, until the tofu is golden and crispy.

6. Meanwhile, steam the broccoli until tender and toss with olive oil, salt, and pepper.

7. Serve the sesame-crusted tofu over cooked brown rice, with steamed broccoli on the side.

8. Garnish with sliced green onions and additional sesame seeds.

Tip: For added flavor, drizzle the tofu with a little extra soy sauce or a sprinkle of chili flakes.

STUFFED PORTOBELLO MUSHROOMS
Prep: 15 Minutes | Cook: 12 Minutes | Makes: 4 Servings

Ingredients:
- 4 large Portobello mushrooms, stems removed and gills scraped out
- 1 cup spinach, chopped
- 1/2 cup ricotta cheese
- 1/4 cup sun-dried tomatoes, chopped
- 1/4 cup shredded mozzarella cheese
- 2 tbsp pine nuts (optional)
- 1 clove garlic, minced
- 1 tbsp olive oil
- Salt and pepper to taste
- Fresh basil for garnish

Directions:
1. Preheat your Breville Smart Oven Air Fryer Pro to 375°F using the Air Fry function.

2. In a skillet, heat the olive oil over medium heat. Add the minced garlic and chopped spinach, sautéing until the spinach is wilted.

3. Remove from heat and stir in the ricotta cheese, sun-dried tomatoes, salt, and pepper.

4. Stuff each Portobello mushroom cap with the spinach and ricotta mixture.

5. Sprinkle shredded mozzarella cheese and pine nuts on top.

6. Place the stuffed mushrooms in the air fryer basket and air fry for 10-12 minutes, or until the mushrooms are tender and the cheese is melted and bubbly.

7. Garnish with fresh basil before serving.

Tip: Serve these stuffed mushrooms with a side salad for a light and satisfying meal.

Mediterranean Chickpea Patties

Prep: 15 Minutes | Cook: 25 Minutes | Makes: 4 Servings

Ingredients:

- 1 can (15 oz) chickpeas, drained and rinsed
- 1/4 cup red onion, finely chopped
- 2 cloves garlic, minced
- 1/4 cup fresh parsley, chopped
- 1/4 cup crumbled feta cheese
- 1/4 cup whole wheat breadcrumbs
- 1 egg, beaten
- 1 tsp ground cumin
- 1/2 tsp smoked paprika
- Salt and pepper to taste
- Olive oil spray
- Tzatziki sauce for serving

Directions:

1. Preheat your Breville Smart Oven Air Fryer Pro to 375°F using the Bake function.

2. In a food processor, combine the chickpeas, red onion, garlic, parsley, feta cheese, breadcrumbs, egg, cumin, smoked paprika, salt, and pepper. Pulse until the mixture is well combined but still slightly chunky.

3. Form the mixture into small patties.

4. Place the patties on a greased baking sheet and lightly spray the tops with olive oil.

5. Bake for 20-25 minutes, flipping halfway through, until the patties are golden brown and firm.

6. Serve the chickpea patties with tzatziki sauce on the side.

Tip: These patties are great in pita bread with lettuce and tomatoes for a healthy sandwich.

Sweet Potato Fries with Avocado Dip

Prep: 10 Minutes | Cook: 15 Minutes | Makes: 4 Servings

Ingredients:

- 2 large sweet potatoes, peeled and cut into fries
- 2 tbsp olive oil
- 1 tsp smoked paprika
- 1/2 tsp garlic powder
- 1/2 tsp ground cumin
- Salt and pepper to taste
- 1 ripe avocado, pitted and peeled
- 1/4 cup Greek yogurt
- Juice of 1 lime
- 1 clove garlic, minced
- Fresh cilantro for garnish

Directions:

1. Preheat your Breville Smart Oven Air Fryer Pro to 400°F using the Air Fry function.

2. In a large bowl, toss the sweet potato fries with olive oil, smoked paprika, garlic powder, cumin, salt, and pepper.

3. Place the sweet potato fries in a single layer in the air fryer basket and air fry for 12-15 minutes, shaking the basket halfway through, until crispy and golden.

4. While the fries are cooking, make the avocado dip by mashing the avocado in a bowl and mixing in the Greek yogurt, lime juice, minced garlic, and salt.

5. Serve the sweet potato fries with the avocado dip on the side, garnished with fresh cilantro.

Tip: For a spicy kick, add a pinch of cayenne pepper to the fries before air frying.

Broccoli and Cauliflower Tots

Prep: 15 Minutes | Cook: 12 Minutes | Makes: 4 Servings

Ingredients:

- 1 cup broccoli florets
- 1 cup cauliflower florets
- 1/2 cup shredded cheddar cheese
- 1/4 cup grated Parmesan cheese
- 1/4 cup whole wheat breadcrumbs
- 1 egg, beaten
- 1/2 tsp garlic powder
- Salt and pepper to taste
- Cooking spray

Directions:

1. Preheat your Breville Smart Oven Air Fryer Pro to 375°F using the Air Fry function.

2. Steam the broccoli and cauliflower florets until tender, about 5 minutes. Drain well and let cool slightly.

3. Finely chop the broccoli and cauliflower and place them in a large mixing bowl.

4. Add the shredded cheddar cheese, Parmesan cheese, breadcrumbs, egg, garlic powder, salt, and pepper. Mix until well combined.

5. Form the mixture into small tots.

6. Place the tots in a single layer in the air fryer basket and lightly spray with cooking spray.

7. Air fry for 10-12 minutes, flipping halfway through, until the tots are golden and crispy.

8. Serve immediately as a healthy snack or side dish.

Tip: Serve these tots with a side of marinara or ranch dressing for dipping.

CRAB STUFFED MUSHROOMS

Prep: 20 Minutes | Cook: 12 Minutes | Makes: 12 Stuffed Mushrooms

Ingredients:

- 12 large white or cremini mushrooms, stems removed
- 4 oz cream cheese, softened
- 1/2 cup cooked crab meat
- 1/4 cup shredded mozzarella cheese
- 2 tbsp grated Parmesan cheese
- 1 clove garlic, minced
- 1 tbsp fresh parsley, chopped
- 1 tsp lemon juice
- Salt and pepper to taste
- Cooking spray

Directions:

1. Preheat your Breville Smart Oven Air Fryer Pro to 375°F using the Air Fry function.

2. In a mixing bowl, combine the cream cheese, crab meat, mozzarella, Parmesan, minced garlic, parsley, lemon juice, salt, and pepper.

3. Spoon the crab mixture into each mushroom cap, pressing down gently to fill.

4. Lightly spray the tops with cooking spray.

5. Place the stuffed mushrooms in the air fryer basket in a single layer.

6. Air fry for 10-12 minutes, or until the mushrooms are tender and the filling is golden and bubbly.

7. Serve warm as an elegant appetizer.

Tip: Garnish with additional chopped parsley or a sprinkle of paprika for color.

MAPLE-GLAZED HOLIDAY HAM

Prep: 15 Minutes | Cook: 1 Hour | Makes: 8-10 Servings

Ingredients:

- 1 fully cooked spiral-cut ham (5-6 lbs)
- 1/2 cup pure maple syrup
- 1/4 cup Dijon mustard
- 1/4 cup brown sugar
- 1 tbsp apple cider vinegar
- 1/2 tsp ground cinnamon
- 1/4 tsp ground cloves
- Pineapple rings and maraschino cherries for garnish (optional)

Directions:

1. Preheat your Breville Smart Oven Air Fryer Pro to 325°F using the Bake function.

2. In a small saucepan, combine the maple syrup, Dijon mustard, brown sugar, apple cider vinegar, cinnamon, and cloves. Heat over medium-low, stirring until the sugar is dissolved.

3. Place the ham in a baking dish and brush the glaze over the top, getting it between the slices as much as possible.

4. Cover the ham loosely with foil and bake for 45 minutes, basting with the glaze every 15 minutes.

5. Remove the foil and bake for an additional 15 minutes, or until the ham is heated through and the glaze is caramelized.

6. Garnish with pineapple rings and cherries if desired, and serve warm.

Tip: Serve this holiday ham with mashed potatoes and roasted vegetables for a complete feast.

BACON-WRAPPED DATES STUFFED

Prep: 10 Minutes | Cook: 10 Minutes | Makes: 16 Stuffed Dates

Ingredients:

- 16 Medjool dates, pitted
- 4 oz goat cheese
- 8 slices bacon, cut in half
- 16 toothpicks

Directions:

1. Preheat your Breville Smart Oven Air Fryer Pro to 375°F using the Air Fry function.
2. Carefully stuff each pitted date with a small amount of goat cheese.
3. Wrap each stuffed date with a half slice of bacon, securing with a toothpick.
4. Place the bacon-wrapped dates in the air fryer basket, making sure they don't touch.
5. Air fry for 8-10 minutes, or until the bacon is crispy and the dates are caramelized.
6. Serve warm as a sweet and savory appetizer.

Tip: Drizzle with honey or balsamic glaze before serving for an extra layer of flavor.

BRIE WITH CRANBERRY SAUCE AND PECANS

Prep: 10 Minutes | Cook: 15 Minutes | Makes: 6-8 Servings

Ingredients:

- 1 wheel of Brie cheese (8 oz)
- 1/2 cup cranberry sauce (homemade or store-bought)
- 1/4 cup pecans, toasted and chopped
- 1 tbsp honey
- Fresh thyme for garnish
- Crackers or sliced baguette for serving

Directions:

1. Preheat your Breville Smart Oven Air Fryer Pro to 350°F using the Bake function.
2. Place the Brie on a parchment-lined baking sheet.
3. Spread the cranberry sauce evenly over the top of the Brie.
4. Sprinkle with chopped pecans and drizzle with honey.
5. Bake for 12-15 minutes, or until the Brie is warm and gooey.
6. Garnish with fresh thyme and serve with crackers or sliced baguette.

Tip: This elegant appetizer is perfect for holiday gatherings and pairs beautifully with a glass of wine.

Holiday Spiced Nuts
Prep: 5 Minutes | Cook: 10 Minutes | Makes: 4 Cups

Ingredients:
- 1 cup almonds
- 1 cup pecans
- 1 cup walnuts
- 1 cup cashews
- 2 tbsp olive oil or melted coconut oil
- 1/4 cup maple syrup
- 1 tsp ground cinnamon
- 1/2 tsp ground ginger
- 1/4 tsp ground nutmeg
- 1/4 tsp ground cloves
- Pinch of salt

Directions:
1. Preheat your Breville Smart Oven Air Fryer Pro to 350°F using the Air Fry function.
2. In a large bowl, toss the nuts with olive oil, maple syrup, cinnamon, ginger, nutmeg, cloves, and salt until well coated.
3. Spread the nuts in a single layer in the air fryer basket.
4. Air fry for 8-10 minutes, shaking the basket halfway through, until the nuts are golden and fragrant.
5. Let the nuts cool completely before serving or storing in an airtight container.

Tip: These spiced nuts make a great holiday gift or snack for entertaining guests.

Prosciutto–Wrapped Asparagus
Prep: 10 Minutes | Cook: 10 Minutes | Makes: 8 Servings

Ingredients:
- 16 asparagus spears, trimmed
- 8 slices prosciutto, halved lengthwise
- 1 tbsp olive oil
- Freshly ground black pepper
- Grated Parmesan cheese for garnish (optional)

Directions:
1. Preheat your Breville Smart Oven Air Fryer Pro to 375°F using the Air Fry function.
2. Wrap each asparagus spear with a half slice of prosciutto.
3. Lightly brush the wrapped asparagus with olive oil and season with freshly ground black pepper.
4. Place the asparagus in a single layer in the air fryer basket.
5. Air fry for 8-10 minutes, or until the prosciutto is crispy and the asparagus is tender.
6. Garnish with grated Parmesan cheese if desired, and serve warm.

Tip: This elegant appetizer is perfect for holiday gatherings and pairs well with a glass of sparkling wine.

Fig Jam Puff Pastry Bites

Prep: 15 Minutes | Cook: 15 Minutes | Makes: 24 Bites

Ingredients:

- 1 sheet puff pastry, thawed
- 4 oz Brie cheese, cut into small cubes
- 1/4 cup fig jam
- 1 egg, beaten (for egg wash)
- Fresh thyme for garnish

Directions:

1. Preheat your Breville Smart Oven Air Fryer Pro to 375°F using the Bake function.
2. Roll out the puff pastry on a floured surface and cut into 24 small squares.
3. Place a cube of Brie and a small dollop of fig jam in the center of each square.
4. Fold the corners of the puff pastry squares over the filling to form a little package.
5. Place the puff pastry bites on a parchment-lined baking sheet and brush the tops with the beaten egg.
6. Bake for 12-15 minutes, or until the puff pastry is golden and puffed.
7. Garnish with fresh thyme and serve warm.

Tip: These bites can be made ahead and baked just before serving for an easy and impressive appetizer.

Coconut Shrimp with Mango Dipping

Prep: 15 Minutes | Cook: 10 Minutes | Makes: 4 Servings

Ingredients:

- 1 lb large shrimp, peeled and deveined, tails on
- 1/2 cup all-purpose flour
- 2 large eggs, beaten
- 1 cup shredded coconut
- 1/2 cup panko breadcrumbs
- 1/4 tsp cayenne pepper
- Salt and pepper to taste
- Cooking spray

For the Mango Dipping Sauce:

- 1 ripe mango, peeled and diced
- 1/4 cup Greek yogurt
- 1 tbsp lime juice
- 1 tsp honey
- Pinch of salt

Directions:

1. Preheat your Breville Smart Oven Air Fryer Pro to 375°F using the Air Fry function.
2. In a shallow dish, mix the shredded coconut, panko breadcrumbs, cayenne pepper, salt, and pepper.
3. Dredge each shrimp in flour, dip in the beaten eggs, and then coat with the coconut mixture.
4. Place the coconut shrimp in a single layer in the air fryer basket and lightly spray with cooking spray.
5. Air fry for 8-10 minutes, flipping halfway through, until the shrimp are golden and crispy.

6. To make the mango dipping sauce, blend the diced mango, Greek yogurt, lime juice, honey, and salt until smooth.

7. Serve the coconut shrimp with the mango dipping sauce on the side.

Tip: This tropical appetizer is a crowd-pleaser and perfect for holiday parties.

BUTTERNUT SQUASH AND SAGE CROSTINI

Prep: 15 Minutes | Cook: 20 Minutes | Makes: 12 Crostini

Ingredients:

- 1 small butternut squash, peeled, seeded, and diced
- 2 tbsp olive oil
- 1 tsp ground cinnamon
- Salt and pepper to taste
- 12 slices of baguette
- 4 oz goat cheese, softened
- 1 tbsp honey
- Fresh sage leaves for garnish

Directions:

1. Preheat your Breville Smart Oven Air Fryer Pro to 375°F using the Bake function.
2. Toss the diced butternut squash with olive oil, cinnamon, salt, and pepper.
3. Spread the squash on a baking sheet and bake for 20 minutes, or until tender and caramelized.
4. Toast the baguette slices in the air fryer for 2-3 minutes until golden.
5. Spread a layer of goat cheese on each toasted baguette slice.
6. Top with the roasted butternut squash and drizzle with honey.
7. Garnish with fresh sage leaves and serve warm.

Tip: These crostini are a great starter for a holiday dinner or festive gathering.

POMEGRANATE GLAZED BRUSSELS SPROUTS

Prep: 10 Minutes | Cook: 12 Minutes | Makes: 4-6 Servings

Ingredients:

- 1 lb Brussels sprouts, trimmed and halved
- 2 tbsp olive oil
- Salt and pepper to taste
- 1/4 cup pomegranate juice
- 1 tbsp balsamic vinegar
- 1 tbsp honey
- Pomegranate arils for garnish
- Chopped toasted pecans for garnish

Directions:

1. Preheat your Breville Smart Oven Air Fryer Pro to 375°F using the Air Fry function.
2. Toss the Brussels sprouts with olive oil, salt, and pepper.
3. Place the Brussels sprouts in a single layer in the air fryer basket and air fry for 10-12 minutes, shaking the basket halfway through, until crispy and golden.

4. In a small saucepan, combine the pomegranate juice, balsamic vinegar, and honey. Simmer over medium heat until reduced by half and thickened.

5. Toss the crispy Brussels sprouts in the pomegranate glaze.

6. Garnish with pomegranate arils and chopped toasted pecans before serving.

Tip: This side dish adds a pop of color and flavor to any holiday table.

HERB AND GARLIC POTATO STACKS
Prep: 15 Minutes | Cook: 25 Minutes | Makes: 6 Servings

Ingredients:

- 4 large potatoes, thinly sliced (use a mandoline for even slices)
- 3 tbsp melted butter
- 2 cloves garlic, minced
- 1 tsp fresh thyme leaves
- 1 tsp fresh rosemary, chopped
- Salt and pepper to taste
- Grated Parmesan cheese for garnish (optional)
- Fresh parsley for garnish

Directions:

1. Preheat your Breville Smart Oven Air Fryer Pro to 375°F using the Air Fry function.

2. In a large bowl, toss the potato slices with melted butter, garlic, thyme, rosemary, salt, and pepper.

3. Stack the potato slices into small piles and place them in a greased muffin tin or individual ramekins.

4. Air fry for 20-25 minutes, or until the potato stacks are golden and crispy on the edges.

5. Remove the stacks from the muffin tin and sprinkle with grated Parmesan cheese if desired.

6. Garnish with fresh parsley and serve warm.

Tip: These potato stacks are a beautiful and delicious side dish for any holiday meal.

CRANBERRY AND BRIE PHYLLO CUPS
Prep: 15 Minutes | Cook: 10 Minutes | Makes: 12 Phyllo Cups

Ingredients:

- 12 phyllo cups (store-bought or homemade)
- 4 oz Brie cheese, cut into small cubes
- 1/4 cup cranberry sauce (homemade or store-bought)
- 1/4 cup chopped pecans, toasted
- Fresh thyme leaves for garnish

Directions:

1. Preheat your Breville Smart Oven Air Fryer Pro to 350°F using the Bake function.

2. Place a cube of Brie in the bottom of each phyllo cup.

3. Top each with a small spoonful of cranberry sauce and a sprinkle of toasted pecans.

4. Bake for 8-10 minutes, or until the Brie is melted and the phyllo cups are golden and crisp.

5. Garnish with fresh thyme leaves and serve warm.

Tip: These bite-sized appetizers are perfect for holiday parties and can be made in advance and baked just before serving.

Rosemary and Lemon Marinated Chicken

Prep: 20 Minutes (plus marinating time) | Cook: 15 Minutes | Makes: 8 Skewers

Ingredients:
- 1 lb chicken breast, cut into bite-sized pieces
- 2 tbsp olive oil
- Juice and zest of 1 lemon
- 2 cloves garlic, minced
- 2 tbsp fresh rosemary, chopped
- Salt and pepper to taste
- 8 wooden skewers, soaked in water for 30 minutes

Directions:
1. In a large bowl, mix together the olive oil, lemon juice, lemon zest, garlic, rosemary, salt, and pepper.
2. Add the chicken pieces to the marinade, tossing to coat. Cover and refrigerate for at least 1 hour, or overnight for more flavor.
3. Preheat your Breville Smart Oven Air Fryer Pro to 375°F using the Air Fry function.
4. Thread the marinated chicken pieces onto the soaked wooden skewers.
5. Place the skewers in a single layer in the air fryer basket.
6. Air fry for 12-15 minutes, turning halfway through, until the chicken is cooked through and lightly charred.
7. Serve the skewers warm with a side of lemon wedges.

Tip: These skewers are great as an appetizer or as part of a holiday buffet.

Pear and Blue Cheese Tart

Prep: 20 Minutes | Cook: 20 Minutes | Makes: 8 Servings

Ingredients:
- 1 sheet puff pastry, thawed
- 2 ripe pears, thinly sliced
- 1/2 cup crumbled blue cheese
- 1/4 cup chopped walnuts, toasted
- 1 tbsp honey
- Fresh thyme leaves for garnish

Directions:
1. Preheat your Breville Smart Oven Air Fryer Pro to 375°F using the Bake function.
2. Roll out the puff pastry on a floured surface and place it on a parchment-lined baking sheet.
3. Arrange the pear slices in an overlapping pattern on top of the puff pastry, leaving a small border around the edges.
4. Sprinkle the crumbled blue cheese and toasted walnuts over the pears.
5. Fold the edges of the puff pastry up and over the filling, pinching to seal the corners.
6. Bake for 18-20 minutes, or until the pastry is golden and puffed.

7. Drizzle with honey and garnish with fresh thyme leaves before serving.

Tip: This tart makes a lovely appetizer or a light dessert for holiday gatherings.

Spiced Apple Chips
Prep: 10 Minutes | Cook: 15 Minutes | Makes: 4 Servings

Ingredients:

- 2 large apples, thinly sliced (use a mandoline for even slices)
- 1 tbsp coconut oil, melted
- 1 tsp ground cinnamon
- 1/4 tsp ground nutmeg
- 1 tbsp maple syrup (optional)

Directions:

1. Preheat your Breville Smart Oven Air Fryer Pro to 300°F using the Air Fry function.
2. In a large bowl, toss the apple slices with melted coconut oil, cinnamon, nutmeg, and maple syrup (if using).
3. Arrange the apple slices in a single layer in the air fryer basket.
4. Air fry for 12-15 minutes, flipping halfway through, until the apple slices are crispy and lightly browned.
5. Let the apple chips cool completely before serving.

Tip: These spiced apple chips are a healthy and festive snack that's perfect for holiday gatherings.

Parmesan and Herb Cheese Straws
Prep: 15 Minutes | Cook: 12 Minutes | Makes: 20 Cheese Straws

Ingredients:
- 1 sheet puff pastry, thawed
- 1/2 cup grated Parmesan cheese
- 1 tsp dried Italian herbs (such as oregano, basil, and thyme)
- 1/2 tsp garlic powder
- 1/4 tsp black pepper
- 1 egg, beaten (for egg wash)

Directions:

1. Preheat your Breville Smart Oven Air Fryer Pro to 375°F using the Air Fry function.
2. Roll out the puff pastry on a lightly floured surface to smooth out any creases.
3. Brush the puff pastry with the beaten egg.
4. In a small bowl, mix together the Parmesan cheese, Italian herbs, garlic powder, and black pepper.
5. Sprinkle the cheese mixture evenly over the puff pastry.
6. Cut the puff pastry into thin strips about 1/2 inch wide.
7. Twist each strip a few times to form a spiral and place them in a single layer in the air fryer basket.
8. Air fry for 10-12 minutes, or until the cheese straws are golden and crispy.
9. Serve warm or at room temperature.

Tip: These cheese straws are perfect for snacking or as an elegant addition to a holiday cheese board.

Goat Cheese and Honey Crostini

Prep: 10 Minutes | Cook: 10 Minutes | Makes: 12 Crostini

Ingredients:

- 1 baguette, sliced into 12 pieces
- 4 oz goat cheese, softened
- 2 tbsp honey
- 1/4 cup chopped walnuts, toasted
- Fresh rosemary or thyme leaves for garnish

Directions:

1. Preheat your Breville Smart Oven Air Fryer Pro to 350°F using the Bake function.
2. Place the baguette slices on a baking sheet and toast them in the air fryer for 3-5 minutes until golden and crispy.
3. Spread a generous amount of goat cheese on each toasted baguette slice.
4. Drizzle with honey and sprinkle with toasted walnuts.
5. Garnish with fresh rosemary or thyme leaves before serving.

Tip: This crostini is an elegant and easy appetizer, perfect for holiday gatherings.

Coconut and Almond-Crusted Chicken Tenders

Prep: 15 Minutes | Cook: 12 Minutes | Makes: 4-6 Servings

Ingredients:

- 1 lb chicken tenders
- 1/2 cup shredded coconut (unsweetened)
- 1/2 cup almond flour
- 1/4 cup panko breadcrumbs
- 1/2 tsp smoked paprika
- 1/2 tsp garlic powder
- Salt and pepper
- 2 large eggs, beaten
- Cooking spray
- Honey mustard or sweet chili sauce for serving

Directions:

1. Preheat Breville Air Fryer to 375°F (Air Fry).
2. Mix coconut, almond flour, breadcrumbs, paprika, garlic powder, salt, and pepper.
3. Dredge chicken in eggs, then coat with the coconut mixture.
4. Place in air fryer, spray with cooking spray, and air fry for 10-12 minutes, flipping halfway.
5. Serve with honey mustard or sweet chili sauce.

Tip: These chicken tenders are a crowd-pleasing appetizer or main dish for holiday entertaining.

Cranberry and Orange Glazed Meatballs

Prep: 20 Minutes | Cook: 20 Minutes | Makes: 24 Meatballs

Ingredients:

- 1 lb ground turkey or beef
- 1/4 cup breadcrumbs
- 1/4 cup Parmesan cheese, grated
- 1 egg, beaten
- 2 cloves garlic, minced
- 1/2 tsp cinnamon
- 1/2 tsp nutmeg
- Salt and pepper
- 1/2 cup cranberry sauce
- 1/4 cup orange juice
- 1 tbsp honey
- 1 tbsp Dijon mustard
- Fresh parsley for garnish

Directions:

1. Preheat Breville Air Fryer to 375°F (Bake).
2. Mix ground meat, breadcrumbs, Parmesan, egg, garlic, cinnamon, nutmeg, salt, and pepper.
3. Roll into meatballs and bake for 15-20 minutes.
4. In a saucepan, simmer cranberry sauce, orange juice, honey, and Dijon mustard until thickened.
5. Toss baked meatballs in glaze and garnish with parsley.

Tip: These festive meatballs are a perfect holiday appetizer or addition to a buffet table.

Holiday Spiced Pear Chips

Prep: 10 Minutes | Cook: 15 Minutes | Makes: 4 Servings

Ingredients:

- 2 large pears, thinly sliced (use a mandoline for even slices)
- 1 tbsp coconut oil, melted
- 1 tsp ground cinnamon
- 1/2 tsp ground ginger
- 1/4 tsp ground cloves
- 1 tbsp maple syrup (optional)

Directions:

1. Preheat your Breville Air Fryer to 200°F (Dehydrate).
2. Lay pear slices on the air fryer rack in a single layer.
3. Sprinkle with cinnamon and nutmeg. Drizzle honey if desired.
4. Dehydrate for 2 hours, flipping halfway, until pears are crispy.
5. Let cool and serve or package for gifting.

Tip: These spiced pear chips are a healthy and festive snack, perfect for holiday gatherings or gift-giving!

APPENDIX I: MEASUREMENT CONVERSION CHART

VOLUME EQUIVALENTS (DRY)

US STANDARD	METRIC (APPROXIMATE)
1/8 teaspoon	0.5 mL
1/4 teaspoon	1 mL
1/2 teaspoon	2 mL
3/4 teaspoon	4 mL
1 teaspoon	5 mL
1 tablespoon	15 mL
1/4 cup	59 mL
1/2 cup	118 mL
3/4 cup	177 mL
1 cup	235 mL
2 cups	475 mL
3 cups	700 mL
4 cups	1 L

VOLUME EQUIVALENTS(LIQUID)

US STANDARD	US STANDARD (OUNCE)	METRIC (APPROXIMATE)
2 tablespoons	1 fl.oz.	30 mL
1/4 cup	2 fl.oz.	60 mL
1/2 cup	4 fl.oz.	120 mL
1 cup	8 fl.oz.	240 mL
1 1/2 cup	12 fl.oz.	355 mL
2 cups or 1 pint	16 fl.oz.	475 mL
4 cups or 1 quart	32 fl.oz.	1 L
1 gallon	128 fl.oz.	4 L

TEMPERATURES EQUIVALENTS

FAHRENHEIT(F)	CELSIUS(C)
225°F	107 °C
250°F	120 °C
275°F	135 °C
300°F	150 °C
325°F	160 °C
350°F	180 °C
375°F	190 °C
400°F	205°C
425°F	220°C
450°F	235 °C
475°F	245 °C
500°F	260 °C

WEIGHT EQUIVALENTS

US STANDARD	METRIC (APPROXIMATE)
1 ounce	28 g
2 ounces	57 g
5 ounces	142 g
10 ounces	284 g
15 ounces	425 g
16 ounces / 1 lb.	454 g
32 ounces / 2 lb.	907 g
2.2 lb.	1kg

INDEX

A

Apple Cinnamon Pancake Bites...........................10
Apple Crisp with Oat Topping............................68
Avocado Fries...28
Avocado Toast with Poached Egg..........................8

B

Bacon-Wrapped Dates Stuffed............................91
Bacon-Wrapped Jalapeño Shrimp.........................30
Baked Banana and Oat Bars...............................18
Baked Berry Cobbler..69
Baked Berry Oatmeal Cups.................................9
Baked Caramel Apple Crumble............................74
Baked Eggs in Avocado....................................13
Baked Empanadas...21
Baked Greek Yogurt and Berry Parfaits.................12
Baked Ham and Cheese Breakfast Sliders..............16
Baked Lemon Herb Quinoa Salad.........................83
Baked Mediterranean Cod with Lemon...................81
Baked Quinoa Breakfast Cups.............................14
Banana Fritters with Honey Drizzle.......................70
Banana Nut Muffins..10
BBQ Glazed Meatloaf.......................................45
Beef and Mushroom Stroganoff...........................44
Beef Kofta with Tzatziki...................................48
Blueberry Pancake Bites...................................15
Breakfast Burritos...9
Breakfast Egg Rolls...19
Breakfast Pizza...12
Breakfast Quesadillas......................................15
Brie Bites with Cranberry Sauce.........................29
Brie with Cranberry Sauce and Pecans..................91
Broccoli and Cauliflower Tots.............................88
Brussels Sprouts with Balsamic Glaze...................57
Buffalo Cauliflower Bites...................................25
Butternut Squash and Sage Crostini......................94

C

Cajun Shrimp and Sausage Skewers......................43
Caprese Stuffed Portobello Mushrooms..................29
Caramelized Onion and Goat Cheese Tartlets..........63
Cauliflower Buffalo Bites...................................83
Cheddar and Chive Biscuits................................57
Cheesy Cauliflower Gratin..................................64
Cheesy Garlic Pull-Apart Bread...........................60
Cheesy Jalapeño Cornbread Muffins......................34
Chia Seed Pudding with Roasted Fruit...................21
Chicken and Broccoli Alfredo..............................50
Chicken and Waffles with Maple Butter..................46
Chicken Cordon Bleu..53
Chicken Fajitas..51
Chicken Parmesan with Marinara.........................41
Chickpea Falafel Bites......................................31
Chocolate Bread Pudding...................................75
Chocolate Lava Cakes......................................70
Churro Waffles..11
Cinnamon Roll Bites..13
Cinnamon Sugar Churro Bites.............................68

Coconut and Almond-Crusted Chicken Tenders.......98
Coconut Macaroons...71
Coconut Shrimp...26
Coconut Shrimp with Mango Dipping.....................93
Coconut-Crusted Avocado Fries..........................36
Coconut-Crusted Chicken Tenders.......................52
Corn Casserole with Cheddar and Jalapeños...........62
Crab Stuffed Mushrooms...................................90
Cranberry and Brie Phyllo Cups..........................95
Cranberry and Orange Glazed Meatballs................99
Crispy Green Beans with Lemon Zest....................61
Crispy Polenta Fries..65
Crispy Sweet Potato Hash with Bacon.....................8
Crispy Tofu Stir-Fry..40
Croissant Sandwiches......................................20

E

Eggplant Parmesan...54
Eggplant Rollatini...51

F

Falafel with Tahini Sauce..................................79
Feta and Tomato Dip.......................................27
Fig Jam Puff Pastry Bites..................................93
French Toast Sticks...14

G

Garlic and Herb Cauliflower Steaks......................82
Garlic Butter Mushrooms...................................65
Garlic Parmesan Asparagus................................56
Goat Cheese and Honey Crostini..........................98
Goat Cheese and Honey Stuffed Dates...................32
Goat Cheese Crostini.......................................28
Granola-Stuffed Apples.....................................17

H

Herb and Garlic Potato Stacks............................95
Herb-Crusted Salmon with Asparagus....................47
Herb-Roasted Baby Potatoes..............................62
Holiday Spiced Nuts..92
Holiday Spiced Pear Chips.................................99
Honey Glazed Carrots with Thyme........................61
How to Use the Breville Smart Oven Pro...................5

J

Jalapeño Poppers..25

L

Lemon Blueberry Scones...................................74
Lemon Garlic Shrimp and Asparagus.....................45
Lemon Garlic Shrimp Skewers.............................53
Lemon Herb Chicken..38
Lemon Herb Chicken with Roasted Vegetables.........79
Lemon Ricotta Cheesecake Bars..........................72

M

Maple Bacon Brussels Sprouts 64
Maple Glazed Carrots 58
Maple Pecan French Toast Casserole.................. 20
Maple-Glazed Holiday Ham 90
Mediterranean Chicken with Olives 43
Mediterranean Chickpea Patties 87
Mediterranean Flatbread 22
Mediterranean Stuffed Tomatoes 59
Moroccan-Spiced Chicken Thighs...................... 47
Mozzarella Stuffed Meatballs 33

N

Nutella-Stuffed Pastry Twists 69

P

Parmesan and Herb Cheese Straws..................... 97
Parmesan Crusted Cauliflower........................... 59
Parmesan Truffle Potato Wedges 32
Peach Hand Pies... 72
Pear and Blue Cheese Tart 96
Pears with Cinnamon and Walnuts 71
Pesto-Crusted Salmon...................................... 50
Pineapple Coconut Upside-Down Cake............... 76
Pomegranate Glazed Brussels Sprouts................ 94
Pork Chops with Apple Cider Glaze.................... 39
Pork Schnitzel with Lemon Caper Sauce.............. 49
Pork Tenderloin with Garlic Herb Rub 41
Prosciutto-Wrapped Asparagus.......................... 92

Q

Quinoa-Stuffed Bell Peppers 78

R

Ratatouille with Balsamic Glaze......................... 42
Rosemary and Lemon Marinated Chicken 96

S

Salmon with Avocado Salsa............................... 78
Salmon with Honey Soy Glaze........................... 39
Sesame-Crusted Tofu with Steamed Broccoli 85
Spiced Apple Chips.. 97
Spicy Chickpea and Avocado Salad..................... 82
Spicy Sriracha Cauliflower Bites 34
Spinach and Artichoke Dip 24
Spinach and Artichoke Gratin............................ 63
Spinach and Feta Pockets.................................. 19
Spinach and Feta Stuffed Phyllo Cups.................. 30
Spinach and Ricotta Stuffed Shells..................... 49
Spinach Artichoke Stuffed Crescent Rolls............ 33
Strawberry Cheesecake Chimichangas.................. 73
Strawberry Stuffed French Toast 22
Stuffed Bell Peppers 18
Stuffed Bell Peppers with Ground Turkey............. 38
Stuffed Mini Bell Peppers................................. 31
Stuffed Mushrooms... 27
Stuffed Portobello Mushrooms 86
Sweet Potato and Black Bean Quesadillas.............. 35
Sweet Potato and Black Bean Salad 66
Sweet Potato and Black Bean Tacos 16

Sweet Potato and Kale Frittata........................... 85
Sweet Potato Chips 26
Sweet Potato Fries with Avocado Dip 87
Sweet Potato Wedges with Cinnamon 56

T

Taquitos.. 17
Teriyaki Chicken Skewers 35
Teriyaki Salmon 54
Tofu and Vegetable Stir-Fry 80

V

Veggie Breakfast Frittata.................................. 11

Z

Zucchini Chips with Garlic Aioli......................... 58
Zucchini Fries 24
Zucchini Noodles with Pesto 80
Zucchini Parmesan Chips 84

Made in the USA
Columbia, SC
21 December 2024